VGM Opportunities Series

OPPORTUNITIES IN BIOTECHNOLOGY CAREERS

Sheldon S. Brown

Revised by
Mark Rowh

Foreword by
Carl B. Feldbaum
President
Biotechnology Industry Organization

VGM Career Books
NTC/Contemporary Publishing Group

Library of Congress Cataloging-in-Publication Data

Brown, Sheldon S., 1937–
    Opportunities in biotechnology careers / Sheldon S. Brown ; revised by Mark Rowh ; foreword by Carl Feldbaum.
      p.   cm.— (VGM opportunities series)
    ISBN 0-658-00479-4 (cloth) — ISBN 0-658-00480-8 (pbk.)
     1. Biotechnology—Vocational guidance.   I. Title: Biotechnology careers.
II. Rowh, Mark. III. Title. IV. Series.

TP248.215 . B766   2000
660.6'023—dc21

                                            00-43261

Published by VGM Career Books
A division of NTC/Contemporary Publishing Group, Inc.
4255 West Touhy Avenue, Lincolnwood (Chicago), Illinois 60712-1975 U.S.A.
Copyright © 2001 by NTC/Contemporary Publishing Group, Inc.
Printed in the United States of America
International Standard Book Number: 0-658-00479-4 (cloth)
                                          0-658-00480-8 (paper)

01   02   03   04   05   06   LB   15   14   13   12   11   10   9   8   7   6   5   4   3   2   1

DEDICATION

In loving memory of my parents
Rabbi Jacob M. Brown
and
Tillie Brown
I would be blessed
if I could possess a fraction
of their kindness, wisdom, and courage!

CONTENTS

Historical perspective. Branches of biotechnology. Major
areas of scientific research.

Genetic engineering. Monoclonal antibody technology.
Bioprocess technology. Medical advances.

What biotechnologists do. Positions in biotechnology. Daily
activities in the lab. Job categories.

Public relations. Sales. Teaching. Patent law.

ABOUT THE AUTHOR

Sheldon S. Brown, writer-photographer and publicist, has been covering the Detroit metropolitan area ever since he received his B. A. in journalism from Wayne State University in the Motor City in June 1959.

His illustrated articles have appeared in magazines of general interest such as *Parade, Science Digest, Grit, Ford Times, Collector's World, The Rotarian, Popular Photography,* and *The National Enquirer.* He is well known in the business field for his many contributions to specialized publications.

Brown is the author of three previous books including *Your Career in Court Administration.*

His biographical notes were submitted by invitation to *Who's Who in the Midwest, The International Authors and Writers Who's Who, The Working Press of the Nation, Contemporary Authors, Contemporary Journalists,* and *Michigan Authors and Poets.*

FOREWORD

Some people have predicted that when future generations look back, they will refer to the twentieth century as the computer age and the twenty-first century as the age of life sciences. Of course, the accuracy of such predictions remains to be seen, but there is no doubt that we live in an era of enormous potential in biotechnology and related areas.

In recent years, biotechnology—where scientists use living things to achieve practical purposes—has garnered startling headlines and fired the imaginations of people around the world. Achievements such as the cloning of mammals or uncovering new secrets about DNA have put biotechnology in the spotlight.

At the same time, less dramatic advances have amounted to something of a revolution. What once was an area dominated by research but with relatively few real-life applications, now makes an enormous impact on people's lives. In everything from preventing or treating diseases to improving agricultural products, advancements in biotechnology have become more commonplace.

With the increasing importance of biotechnology, more and more companies, research organizations, and other employers depend on the work of appropriately trained professionals to conduct research or perform other functions. This means that for men and women with the right skills, career prospects may be bright indeed.

Can you picture yourself helping develop a new medicine or vaccine for a currently incurable disease based on biotechnology principles? How would you feel about making fruits or vegetables more nutritious, longer lasting, or more resistant to insects or disease? Would you find it satisfying to serve on a team cleaning up a hazardous waste site and turning it into safe, productive land? Can you see yourself conducting research in an area such as molecular biology or gene therapy? Professionals who work in biotechnology perform these tasks and many others.

Certainly, pursuing a career in biotechnology requires hard work and dedication. At the same time, it can offer significant rewards. The chance to do challenging work that helps improve the human condition is nothing to take lightly.

Opportunities in Biotechnology Careers presents both an overview of the field and a clear look at the some of the specific jobs that can be found.

If an occupation in this area sounds appealing, please read further and check things out. Who knows? Perhaps a career in biotechnology awaits you.

> Carl B. Feldbaum
> President
> Biotechnology Industry Organization

ACKNOWLEDGMENTS

The author deeply appreciates all the individuals and organizations who contributed to this book, including the following:

David Jensen
Daniel and Sharon Brown
Ms. Charlene J. Coursen
Biotechnology Industry Organization, Washington, DC
Montgomery County High Technology Council, Inc.
North Carolina Biotechnology Center
Dr. Dave Smith
Dr. Mark Bloom
Ms. Susan Saraquse
Dr. Harish Padh
B.C. Biotechnology Alliance
Ms. Lisa Idry
Massachusetts Biotechnology Council
Ms. Sarah Manning
Marina Knez

INTRODUCTION

A couple of decades ago, biotechnology was hardly an industry at all. People with training in the life sciences typically pursued careers in medicine or academia, with few other options. Today, with hundreds of new biotechnology companies and academic programs, there are innumerable career options, scientific and nonscientific, for anyone interested in the life sciences.

Since the first edition of this book was published, many biotechnology firms have shifted their focus from research and development to producing and selling marketable products. Although careers in biotechnology have traditionally required scientific backgrounds, this industry shift has opened up a wider range of job opportunities by creating a greater demand for engineers and people with expertise in nonscientific areas, including managers, marketing personnel, salespeople, lawyers, regulatory specialists, and financial analysts.

Biotechnology has already profoundly changed the quality of our lives through improved medicine, diagnostics, agriculture, and waste management, to name a few of the many areas of this burgeoning industry. Because the field of biotechnology is still growing, there are unique opportunities to forge new territory, make new discoveries, and introduce useful innovations into the marketplace. A career in biotechnology holds great promise for anyone motivated to seek out the proper training. Perhaps this book will help you determine if and how you might fit into the fascinating and continually transforming world of biotechnology.

CHAPTER 1

THE NATURE OF BIOTECHNOLOGY

The field of biotechnology is both new and complex. As a result many people have little, if any, idea what it involves. Some people equate biotechnology with genetically engineered foods such as "bionic" tomatoes that last longer before spoiling; others associate the term with medical breakthroughs such as test-tube babies and new techniques for diagnosing cancer and other diseases. Although these examples do indeed fall under the category of biotechnology, the field encompasses a much wider range of scientific and technological techniques and processes.

We can begin to understand the term *biotechnology* by examining its parts. *Bio* means living organisms or tissue. *Technology* is a scientific method of achieving a practical purpose. Thus, biotechnology, in simple terms, is scientists using living things to achieve practical purposes.

The U.S. government defines biotechnology as "any technique that uses living organisms or parts of living organisms to: (1) make or modify products, (2) improve plants or animals, or (3) develop microorganisms for specific uses."

Other countries define biotechnology slightly differently. For example, the Canadian government's definition is as follows: "Biotechnology is the utilization of a biological process, be it via microbial plant or animal cells, or their constituents, to provide goods and services." And the European Federation defines biotechnology as "the integrated use of biochemistry, microbiology, and engineering sciences in order to achieve industrial application of the capabilities of microorganisms, cultured tissue cells, and parts thereof."

Because of its complexity, the field of biotechnology is, in many ways, still being defined. Biotechnology, as you will learn, has tremendous potential for bettering our lives by providing opportunities to improve health care, agriculture, and our environment. Standing at the frontier of this exciting field, our biggest challenge is to use the power of biotechnology wisely: to carefully consider its implications before bringing about irreversible changes to our planet.

HISTORICAL PERSPECTIVE

Modern biotechnology has roots stretching back to the dawn of humanity. Ten thousand years ago, enterprising ancient peoples learned that they could improve the quality and quantity of certain foods by controlling the conditions of fermentation. They used microorganisms (yeast) to make wine, beer, and bread. Early farmers discovered that they could boost the numbers and improve the taste of their crops by saving and planting the seeds of desirable plants. Crops that gave the highest yield, stayed healthiest during periods of drought or disease, and were the easiest to harvest tended to pass on their favorable characteristics to future generations. Farmers learned that they could perpetuate and even strengthen the desirable traits through several years of careful seed selection.

Centuries later in the mid-1860s, Gregor Mendel discovered the scientific basis of these early farming techniques while studying the hereditary traits of peas. Mendel's work opened the doors to understanding genetic processes and crossbreeding (hybridization). However, only in the twentieth century, with the advantages of sophisticated laboratories and technological equipment, have scientists had a solid understanding of the scientific principles behind natural processes such as fermentation and heredity.

BRANCHES OF BIOTECHNOLOGY

Biotechnology is not a single science, nor is it a single procedure, technique, or process. Rather, it is a field involving a multitude of biotechnological techniques that draw upon all the sciences, as well as engineering. Consequently, there is no single educational track that will prepare a student for a career in biotechnology.

Biotechnology can be grouped into three general categories: (1) human health care, (2) agriculture and animal health care, and (3) energy/environmental management. These categories may be broken down further into the following subcategories:

Applications in human health care:

1. monoclonal antibodies
2. detection and treatment of diseases such as cancer, AIDS, and cardiovascular conditions
3. vaccines
4. human growth and other hormones
5. enzymes
6. other proteins
7. improved and new antibiotics, drugs, and vitamins
8. gene therapy

Applications in agriculture and animal health care:

1. food additives, proteins, enzymes, and vitamins
2. biopesticides and biofertilizers
3. improved crop yield and quality
4. animal feed supplements
5. vaccines
6. plant growth hormones
7. diagnostic reagents for plant and animal diseases
8. transgenic animals
9. microbial nitrogen fixation and manipulation of symbionts

Applications in energy/environmental management:

1. biomass from chemicals, wastes, residues, and fuel crops
2. enhanced oil recovery
3. chemicals and solvents
4. decomposition and detoxification of chemicals
5. biosensors and biochips
6. improved microbial systems for environmental control of air, water, and soil
7. extraction of low-grade metals and recovery of valuable metals
8. hydrogen and carbon dioxide production

MAJOR AREAS OF SCIENTIFIC RESEARCH

Following is a list of some of the major areas of scientific research in which biotechnology companies are involved:

agricultural products
anticancer therapeutics
biocatalysis
biochemical engineering
biosynthesis
cellular biology
chemicals
chromatography
diagnostics
enzymology

fermentation
gene synthesis
genetic engineering
health care products (human and other animals)
human-made fibers
hybridoma technology
immunology
industrial enzymes
minerals
molecular biology
monoclonal antibodies
oil- and gas-related research
pharmaceutical research
plastics
preparatory biologicals
products in gram-positive organisms
protein chemistry
recombinant DNA products and processes
resins
seed inoculants
seeds
sequencing
specialized electronic and process control systems

CHAPTER 2

RECENT DEVELOPMENTS IN BIOTECHNOLOGY

For anyone considering a career in biotechnology, the Biotechnology Industry Organization (BIO) is a vital source of information about the newest developments in the field. Much of the following is based on information provided courtesy of this organization.

GENETIC ENGINEERING

Genetic engineering, or bioengineering, is currently one of the most exciting and publicized branches of biotechnology. Since the development of sophisticated gene splicing in the mid-1970s, a technique known as recombinant DNA, scientists have been able to remove and add genetic material to a cell's DNA. By impregnating the genetic material of plants and animals with "helpful" genes taken from the DNA of other organisms, biotechnologists are creating new kinds of foods, including some that you may soon see on the shelves of your local grocery stores.

7

The United States Department of Agriculture frequently issues permits to companies across the country allowing them to field-test genetically engineered crops. Many bioengineered foods have already been developed, and more are in process.

High-yield agriculture in recent decades has involved the use of vast amounts of fertilizer and pesticide chemicals. These toxic chemicals have a devastating effect on the environment and are extremely costly to farmers. Biotechnologists hope to reduce the need for fertilizers and pesticides by creating plants that can repel pests and help to fertilize themselves. Agronomists also are using genetic engineering to strengthen plants against diseases and harmful environmental conditions such as soil salinity, drought, alkaline, earth metals, and soil that lacks air.

Some of the genetically engineered foods that are currently being tested are a type of rice that has greater protein content, wheat that can help fertilize itself by producing its own nitrogen, tomatoes that have more pulp and less water, and potatoes that absorb less fat when fried. Biotechnologists also are experimenting with using gene splicing to make chickens bigger, pigs leaner, and crops such as strawberries and tomatoes resistant to frost damage.

Ethical Issues

While the possibilities of genetic engineering seem virtually limitless, there are legitimate concerns about this new branch of biotechnology. The power of bioengineering has tremendous potential for good; however, it can just as easily be used irresponsibly. For example, some of the agricultural research currently being conducted is aimed at creating plants with greater resistance to the harmful effects of pesticides. Such crops would still require the use of pesticides and perhaps even encourage greater pesticide usage because of their increased tolerance. Why create plants that can better withstand pesticides when it is possible to create plants that can repel pests themselves, eliminating the need for pesticides? The answer is that chemical companies that sell pesticides want to ensure that farmers will continue to buy their products.

Environmentalists are concerned about what will happen when genetically engineered plants and animals enter earth's delicate ecosystem and food chain. Many people predict that creating genetically altered organisms will further reduce the earth's biological diversity, result in "superweeds" that will threaten current plant species, and produce unforeseen allergens and toxins in the foods we eat. Other people question the morality of manipulating the genetic makeup of animals. What will stop people from using biotechnological methods to manipulate human DNA, controlling who and what will be born?

From a scientific standpoint, bioengineering is an extremely exciting field; however, it has raised difficult questions. Scientists and students interested in this branch of biotechnology will need to consider the social, ethical, and environmental implications of genetic manipulation before attempting to utilize its power.

MONOCLONAL ANTIBODY TECHNOLOGY

Another facet of biotechnology is monoclonal antibody technology. Substances foreign to the body, such as viruses, disease-causing bacteria, and other infectious agents, have structural features jutting from their surfaces. These features, called antigens, are recognized by the body's immune system as invaders. Our natural defenses against these infectious agents are antibodies, proteins that seek out the antigens and help to destroy them.

Antibodies have two very useful characteristics. First, they are extremely specific; that is, each antibody binds to and attacks one particular antigen. Second, some antibodies, once activated by the occurrence of a disease, continue to offer resistance against that disease. For example, once you have had the chicken pox, you should never have it again.

That second characteristic of antibodies makes it possible to create vaccines. A vaccine is a preparation of killed or weakened bacteria or viruses that, when introduced into the body, stimulates the production of antibodies against the antigens it contains.

It is the first trait of antibodies, their specific nature, that makes monoclonal antibody technology so valuable. Not only can antibodies be used therapeutically to protect against disease, they can also help to diagnose a wide variety of illnesses. Furthermore, they can detect the presence of drugs, viral and bacterial products, and other unusual or abnormal substances in the blood.

Because there is such a diversity of uses for these disease-fighting substances, their production in pure quantities has long been the focus of scientific investigation. The conventional method had been to inject a laboratory animal with an antigen and then, when antibodies had been formed, collect those antibodies from the blood serum. There are two problems with this method. It yields antiserum (an antibody containing blood serum), which is comprised of undesired substances. Also, it provides a very small amount of usable antibody.

Monoclonal antibody technology allows scientists to produce large amounts of pure antibodies.

BIOPROCESS TECHNOLOGY

Like other applications of biotechnology, modern bioprocess technology is an extension of ancient techniques for developing useful products by taking advantage of natural biological activities. When our early ancestors made alcoholic beverages, they used a bioprocess—the combination of yeast cells and cereal grains. This combination formed a fermentation system in which the organisms consumed the grain for their own growth and, while doing so, produced by-products (alcohol and carbon dioxide gas) that helped to make the beverage. Although certainly more advanced, today's bioprocess technology is based upon the same principle: combining living matter (whole organisms or enzymes) with nutrients under the conditions necessary to make the desired end product.

Bioprocesses have become widely used in several areas of commercial biotechnology. These include the production of enzymes used for such things as food processing, waste management, and antibodies.

As techniques and instrumentation are refined, bioprocesses may have applications in other areas where chemical processes are now used. They offer several advantages over the latter: bioprocesses require lower temperature, pressure, and pH (a measure of acidity); they can use renewable resources as raw materials; and greater quantities can be produced with less energy consumption.

MEDICAL ADVANCES

AIDS Research

AIDS (Acquired Immune Deficiency Syndrome) is one of the most serious health threats presently facing modern society. Since AIDS was first recognized as a disease in 1983, millions of people around the world have been infected with the human immunodeficiency virus (HIV) that causes AIDS. Too many will die of AIDS unless a cure is found.

Biotechnology has played a crucial role in preventing the spread of AIDS, as well as treating it. Using monoclonal antibody technology, biomedical researchers have developed a laboratory test that shows whether blood has been contaminated with the HIV virus. This has helped slow the spread of AIDS by informing people if they are HIV carriers and enabling hospitals to screen donated blood.

Scientists have experimented in recent years with genetically engineered proteins as possible treatments for HIV and the infectious diseases that accompany it. HIV infection destroys T-4 lymphocytes, which make up an important part of the body's immune system. Without these lymphocytes, the body is vulnerable to a wide range of diseases that it would normally ward off without difficulty. A natural protein called CD4 is found on the surface of the body's T-4 cells and acts as a gate, allowing the virus to enter the cells. By introducing bioengineered CD4 protein into the bloodstream as a decoy, scientists hope that the HIV virus will attack it instead of T-4 cells.

Scientists also are using biotechnology techniques in an effort to develop an AIDS vaccine. Traditionally, vaccines have been made from a dead or weakened virus, which stimulates the body's natural defenses while not actually producing disease. If the immunized person is later infected with the natural virus, his or her stimulated immune system is ready to destroy the invader. A weakened or killed HIV virus, however, can become reactivated and cause AIDS rather than produce immunity. Several biotechnology companies are investigating the idea of using part of the HIV virus to create a vaccine that cannot become reactivated and lead to AIDS. Efforts to develop a vaccine have been thus far unsuccessful, mainly because the virus itself is changing so quickly. Because HIV occurs in several different forms, it is unlikely that a single vaccine will be effective against all of them.

Disease Prevention and Treatment

Biotechnologists are also involved in the fight against disease—both treating and avoiding it. First, they determine what specific drugs are required. Then they plan their design. Experts predict another "explosion" of discoveries leading to many new pharmaceutical products that will far exceed the substantial growth in drug development over the last fifty years.

Professionals in the health field, as well as their patients, already owe much to biotechnology. Vitamin B12, steroids, and many birth control pills originate from biotechnological sources. Human insulin was the first recombinant DNA-derived product to become commercially available. It was first marketed in 1982.

The Biotechnology Industry Organization reports other important studies biotechnologists are making to keep us healthy, including the following:

FIGHTING HEART DISEASE

Heart attacks may occur in people whose arteries have been narrowed by the accumulation of cholesterol. If a blood clot enters one of the coronary arteries, which supply blood to the heart muscle, it can become lodged in a narrowed section of the artery, cutting off blood flow to a portion of the heart muscle. Without quick and effective treatment, the heart can be damaged permanently.

Each year, 1.1 million people suffer heart attacks. More than 400,000 of those attacks are fatal. Many of these patients can be saved from death or permanent disability with a genetically engineered drug called tissue plasminogen activator, or TPA.

TPA is a natural human protein that dissolves blood clots. It occurs naturally in the blood, but in amounts too small to stop a heart attack.

When a heart attack strikes, doctors may inject genetically engineered TPA into the patient's blood. The protein travels to the clot, breaking it up within minutes and restoring blood flow to the heart muscle. By quickly restoring blood flow, TPA helps prevent life-threatening damage to the heart muscle.

The U.S. Food and Drug Administration approved TPA in 1987, and it is available in most hospitals. Eventually, the drug may be used by ambulance crews—or heart patients themselves—to stop heart attacks before the patient even reaches the hospital.

NEW WEAPONS FOR THE WAR ON CANCER

Cancer is an error in cell development. Normal cells grow and reproduce rapidly when they are young and then slow down or stop reproducing when they mature. Somehow cancer cells get tricked into staying immature, and they reproduce wildly.

Despite the nation's war on cancer since the early 1970s, cancer is still second only to heart disease as a killer. Each year, more than one million Americans develop cancer, and more than five hundred thousand people die from the disease.

Biotechnology is used to treat cancer in three ways. Some genetically engineered proteins, called lymphokines, appear to attack cancer cells directly, or they may trigger the body's immune system to attack the cancer. Other genetically engineered proteins, called growth factors, appear to push cancer cells to maturity, slowing the rampant reproduction. And monoclonal antibodies armed with radioactive material, cancer drugs, or other poisons search out and destroy cancer cells.

One genetically engineered lymphokine, alpha-interferon, is used to treat people with hairy cell leukemia, a cancer that several hundred Americans develop each year.

Before alpha-interferon came along, a diagnosis of hairy cell leukemia was a death sentence. People with the disease required frequent blood transfusions and became highly susceptible to infections. There were no effective long-term treatments.

Now, alpha-interferon can restore people with hairy cell leukemia to normal health. The protein appears to bind to the surface of the cancer cell, halting its growth.

In addition to alpha-interferon, doctors are looking to other genetically engineered lymphokines to treat cancer patients. Interleukin-2 activates special white blood cells, called killer cells, that can destroy cancer cells. These activated killer cells may prove to be an effective treatment for people with advanced skin and kidney cancers.

Another group of proteins, called colony stimulating factors, trigger the production and activity of cells of the immune system. Colony stimulating factors may prove useful in marshalling the body's defenses against cancer and AIDS. They may also help restore normal blood production in patients with severe anemia or those undergoing bone marrow transplantation.

OTHER DISEASES

Heart disease, cancer, AIDS, and diabetes are just some of the diseases biotechnology will help to treat in the coming years. Here is a sample of some of the other conditions for which biotechnology products are available or under development:

- **Dwarfism.** Children lacking sufficient growth hormone cannot grow to normal height without regular injections of human growth hormone. Traditionally, these children were treated with limited supplies of growth hormone from cadavers. But in 1985, cadaver-derived hormone was removed from the market after several children died from a rare virus that contaminates it. Unlike cadaver-derived hormone, genetically engineered growth hormone is a safe therapy for treating dwarfism.

- **Hemophilia.** Hemophiliacs are constantly at risk of internal bleeding because their bodies cannot produce enough of a protein called Factor VIII, which controls blood clotting. Transfusions of Factor VIII from human blood can control the disorder, but these transfusions contain only 1 percent Factor VIII and can transmit viral diseases. Some hemophiliacs were infected with the HIV from transfusions in the early 1980s, and they can still get hepatitis from contaminated Factor VIII.

Now, monoclonal antibody technology is being used to make Factor VIII that is 99 percent pure. And studies are underway with genetically engineered Factor VIII, which is completely pure and incapable of transmitting disease.

- **Anemia.** Hundreds of thousands of people suffer each year from anemia associated with a variety of conditions, such as chronic renal failure and AIDS. People on kidney dialysis or undergoing cancer therapy generally suffer from anemia and must receive blood transfusions. As with hemophiliacs, transfusions carry the risk of infectious disease. Several biotechnology companies have developed genetically engineered erythropoietin, a natural human hormone that stimulates the production of red blood cells and may be useful in treating anemia and reducing the need for transfusions.

- **Organ rejection.** When a patient receives a kidney or other transplanted organ, the patient's immune system may recognize it as an invader and attack it. Such rejection can cause a transplant to fail, and in some cases, the rejection can be fatal. Using monoclonal antibodies, doctors can eliminate T cells, elements of the immune system responsible for organ rejection.

- **Common cold.** Medicine has conquered many common bacterial diseases with antibiotics. But antibiotics are useless against viral diseases, such as the common cold. The lymphokine interferon—referred to earlier as the treatment for hairy cell leukemia—may be effective against the virus that causes 40 percent of all colds.

ADVANCES IN DISEASE DIAGNOSIS

All of these powerful new therapies would be of little use if doctors could not accurately determine which diseases or other conditions their patients have. In addition to providing new drugs, biotechnology has added to the physician's trove of diagnostic tools.

A number of biotechnology companies are using monoclonal antibodies in diagnostic tests. Because monoclonal antibodies bind specifically to certain targets, they are generally more effective than conventional diagnostic tools in identifying the cause and location of disease. To cite just a few examples, monoclonal antibodies are used in diagnostic procedures for hepatitis, venereal disease, and bacterial infections. They are also used in home pregnancy test kits.

Doctors can use monoclonal antibodies to "see" into the human body with a clarity unimaginable a decade ago. A physician injects a patient with monoclonal antibodies that carry minute amounts of radioactive material. The antibodies then attach to their target, such as a tumor or heart muscle damaged by a heart attack. The doctor uses a computerized scanning device to locate and study the diseased tissue so that an appropriate course of therapy can be planned.

Recombinant DNA technology allows physicians to identify specific genes, enabling the doctors to diagnose genetic disorders such as cystic fibrosis. Recombinant techniques also are used to detect HIV infection and may someday be used to diagnose a variety of infectious diseases, including cancer.

SOME DISEASES OR AILMENTS THAT MAY BE TREATED OR PREVENTED WITH BIOTECHNOLOGY

anemia
arthritis
chronic granulomatous disease
Crohn's disease
diabetes
female infertility
fungal infections
genital warts
heart attacks
hemophilia
hepatitis
human growth hormone deficiency
influenza
leukemia
Lyme disease
lymphomatous meningitis
multiple sclerosis
rejection of kidney transplants
severe combined immunodeficiency disease (SCID)
several types of cancer

THE NEXT FRONTIER: DISEASE PREVENTION

As amazing as some of the therapeutic and diagnostic uses of biotechnology may seem today, they may someday appear crude. The real promise of the new biology is in helping scientists understand the cause of disease, so that health care professionals will better be able to prevent most diseases.

Biotechnology companies and pharmaceutical firms are developing vaccines against a host of infectious diseases, in addition to AIDS. Doctors now have a genetically engineered vaccine against hepatitis B, for instance, a viral disease that more than two hundred thousand people contract each year.

Genetically engineered vaccines will have the greatest impact in developing nations, where millions die or suffer chronic illness from viral and parasitic diseases such as malaria and schistosomiasis. Scientists may be able to use genetic engineering to mix the genes of many infectious agents, producing a single vaccine that could be used to immunize people in the world's developing countries against a wide range of diseases.

Disease prevention is also an important issue in developed countries. Death from heart disease, for example, can be greatly reduced by lowering the amount of cholesterol-laden food people consume. The risk of cancer can be reduced with a low-fat, high-fiber diet. Biotechnology companies are using genetic engineering to develop foods and food ingredients that are more healthful but still tasty.

Biotechnology also presents the possibility of correcting genetic disorders. Caused by an insufficient amount of a single protein, severe combined immune deficiency is the hereditary disorder brought to public attention by David, the boy in the plastic bubble. Children with this disease cannot fight off simple infections, and they rarely survive the first two years of life. The condition may be cured by replacing the gene that codes for the deficient protein.

Replacing missing or defective genes in a person with a genetic disorder would restore normal function to the individual, but the person could still pass the genetic defect on to his or her children. Some doctors have proposed eliminating genetic defects in reproductive cells to prevent offspring from inheriting the disorder. This step, however, raises ethical questions about who will decide which genes should be passed to future generations.

John Fletcher, Ph.D., professor of biomedical ethics and religious studies at the University of Virginia School of Medicine, Charlottesville, believes human gene therapy can be used without violating ethical principles.

"If you had the power not only to prevent a genetic disorder, but to protect the next generation, would you want to take that step? Most people would say 'yes,'" Fletcher said.

But Fletcher also said that doctors and patients must "keep the line drawn between treating real diseases that cause death and pain and suffering, and trying to engineer perfect people."

Briefly summarizing the feats of a young and robust science is a challenging task. For one thing, new accomplishments come along at a rapid pace. We are living at a time when some of the answers to elusive questions about fundamental biological processess soon may be found with the help of biotechnology. Using more powerful methods than ever before, many of which were only dreamed of a short time ago, biotechnologists are changing our world.

CHAPTER 3

BASICS OF A BIOTECHNOLOGY CAREER

Biotechnology has a definite mystique about it. Most of its concepts were unheard of only a short time ago. Today's version of the science will give way to the yet-unthought-of discoveries of the coming decades. A career in biotechnology can be glamorous, but this romantic field has its mundane side, too. In order for biotechnology firms to operate efficiently, there are somewhat standardized job titles that have well-defined, down-to-earth duties and entry prerequisites. Before spotlighting these specific details, a quick overview of the categories that make up the biotechnological workplace is in order.

WHAT BIOTECHNOLOGISTS DO

Molecular biologists and immunologists constitute about a third of the research workers in biotechnology. Most molecular biologists focus on animal and bacterial systems, because this research is most applicable to human health. Substantial funding for molecular biology comes from the National Institutes of Health. Immunologists are greatly involved in the development of hybridomas (the cells produced by fusing two cells of different origins) to create monoclonal antibodies. More recently, the employment of plant molecular biologists has been increasing, with the redirection of agricultural research toward molecular biological techniques.

Bioprocess engineers, biochemists, and microbiologists develop methods of producing biotechnology products in large quantities. The demand for these specialties will increase as products are readied for production.

Microbiologists study bacteria, yeast, and other microorganisms. They identify microbes with particular characteristics for industrial processes. Microbiologists also identify optimum growth conditions for microorganisms and the conditions for their production.

Cell culture specialists perform similar functions for plant and animal cells grown in tissue culture. Tissue culture is becoming increasingly important for the processing of useful products. Expertise in working with tissue culture is a skill much in demand.

Bioprocess engineers design systems to approximate conditions identified by the microbiologists. Bioprocess engineering is related to chemical engineering. One of the main tasks undertaken by bioprocess engineers is the design of fermentation vats and the various vessels used for bioprocessing (bioreactors) that hold the microorganisms that will produce given products. Bioprocess engineers are required for the next stage of production too—the recovery, purification, and quality control of products. Many of these products are extremely fragile, making purification a difficult and highly demanding job.

POSITIONS IN BIOTECHNOLOGY

The following basic outline provides a general idea of the common positions existing within the biotechnological industry. Companies engaged in biotechnology-related research and development may differ in the employment opportunities they offer, the education and experience histories they expect, and the responsibilities of members of their personnel teams at particular job levels. The following job descriptions highlight one position each from a group of research families. (A family is a collection of jobs that call for the performance of similar types of activities.)

Lab Assistant

A lab assistant I is responsible for performing a variety of research/laboratory tasks and experiments under general supervision. This could involve making detailed observations, analyzing data, and interpreting results in written reports and summaries. Duties also could include maintaining laboratory equipment and inventory levels of supplies.

This job classification usually is filled by graduates from two- or four-year programs that provide minimal backgrounds in biology. Some firms will hire individuals with their high school diplomas or equivalent experience who have a minimum of zero to one year of relevant laboratory background.

Lab assistants are not "gofers." They could have their own projects, although this is not as common a practice in commercial/industrial laboratories as it is in those at universities.

A lab assistant carries out routine, day-to-day laboratory procedures. Many employers realize that lab assistants will be more productive if they do not have to repeat the same activity all the time. Therefore, a lab assistant I can be responsible for a variety of procedures such as preparing the solutions, chemicals, and tools that everyone senior to this job level utilizes. He or she should be considered an important part of the whole laboratory picture.

The number of techniques that lab assistants accomplish as they move up in rank from I to III increases. Prior experience is the factor that counts if someone wants to advance from lab assistant I to lab assistant II. Lab assistant III is the level where a laboratory manager or somebody who has only a bachelor's degree peaks and stops. It is not unusual to find someone settling in at this position for five years or more.

Research Associate

A research associate I is responsible for research and development in collaboration with others for products and projects. He or she makes detailed observations, analyzes data, and interprets results. Someone at this level may exercise technical creativity and discretion in the design, execution, and interpretation of experiments that contribute to projects. A research associate I prepares technical reports and summaries. The job calls for staying familiar with current scientific literature.

People management, specifically of lab assistants, is a responsibility of research associates. For example, only lab assistants, not research associates, have to prepare solutions, chemicals, and DNA and RNA tools for everyone's use.

Remember, however, that the beginning job classifications are very flexible. Some people who would be associates II in one company may be labeled assistant III at another firm. It also is not that unusual to find research associates who are doing more demanding work than those employees who are classified as scientists.

Years of experience, the nature of his or her independent research, and the excellence ratings of his or her experiments are the factors propelling a person up the ladder from associate I to associate IV. While a B.S. in a scientific discipline is often sufficient to start out, those research associates who can anticipate successful career growth plan to earn a Ph.D. degree.

Postdoctoral Research Scientist

A postdoctoral research scientist is responsible for the design, development, execution, and implementation of scientific research involving a large research team. He or she investigates the feasibility of applying a wide variety of scientific principles and theories to patented inventions and products. This biotechnologist maintains extensive knowledge of state-of-the-art principles and theories. A postdoctoral research scientist contributes to scientific literature and conferences.

Obviously, the educational prerequisite for this position is a Ph.D. in a scientific discipline. Employers prefer postdoctoral research scientists to have experience in a research environment. Hiring officials expect job candidates to demonstrate potential for technical proficiency, creativity, cooperative abilities with others, and the knack for independent thought.

As a general rule, a postdoctoral research scientist I is a person who just received his or her Ph.D. A postdoctoral research scientist II is an individual with two to three years of professional experience.

Scientist

A scientist does the same things as a postdoctoral research scientist. In addition, he or she may coordinate interdepartmental activities and research efforts. The scientist uses professional concepts and company policies and procedures to solve a broad range of difficult problems in imaginative and practical ways.

The requirements for scientist I are a B.S. or M.S. in a scientific discipline and preferably one to three or more years of experience in a research environment. A Ph.D. is helpful for advancement and may be required for a scientist I position by some companies. Different companies have different criteria, but, for the most part, several years of on-the-job accomplishments separate the scientist II, scientist III, and scientist IV levels. To move up at all in these levels, a person basically has to show employers what he or she has done and what he or she plans on doing. Some firms use the categories of assistant scientist and full scientist to classify these levels.

Merit often can help a bright scientist advance at a faster pace than normal. If, for example, you are twenty-four years old, just received your Ph.D., and, in one year, you found a clone that is worth a great deal of money for your company, you can disregard the years-on-the-job requirement usually needed for the upgrading of your scientist classification. You probably would become a scientist IV right away, once management officers realized you are an independent starter and can inspire people.

Associate Scientific Director

By the time a person works up to the job of associate scientific director, he or she may actually be leaving the laboratory. In fact, the higher a person goes on this ladder of position titles, supervisory and paperwork tasks will increase and responsibility for working in the laboratory will diminish.

The ultimate transition away from the laboratory bench is at the level of higher scientist or associate scientific director. The chance of anyone working at either of these levels doing any research is minimal.

Associate scientific directors organize and manage groups of people. They establish what their personnel will work on, what directions are or are not functioning well, who to hire or fire, and which individuals have earned promotions. Some companies assign associate scientific directors to specific, individual projects.

Scientific Director

A scientific director is responsible for managing the activities of an entire scientific/engineering group in the research, design, and development of an organization's products, projects, and programs. This biotechnologist conducts and works with others on basic research relevant to long-term objectives and concerns. He or she writes and reviews manuscripts for publication. Other duties involve developing strategies to ensure effective achievement of scientific goals and monitoring and evaluating the completion of tasks and projects. You can find a scientific director putting together budgets for capital expenditures and labor. This official also participates with other top managers to establish company policies. He or she makes the final decisions on administrative or operational matters. It is not unusual for companies to assign different scientific directors for different fields of interest.

A person entertaining thoughts of being a scientific director should consider the following qualifications. He or she needs a Ph.D. in a related scientific discipline. His or her resume should feature a minimum of ten years of related work experience and some management background. The job candidate must be recognized for individual scientific accomplishments. He or she also must be willing to work very hard—sixty-hour workweeks are not abnormal in the biotechnology industry.

Project Manager and Technical Services Manager

Although some experts list the job titles of project manager and technical services manager in the overall research category, other authorities question their presence in this grouping.

A project manager is responsible for providing oversight in order to maximize the effective use of resources. He or she facilitates information flow between research team members, the project leaders, senior management, and the corporate client. The goal of the project manager is to maintain positive interaction with the client and initiate and coordinate the decision-making process. The direction rendered by a project manager is administrative rather than technical. His or her supervision is indirect rather than direct.

The educational prerequisite for this position is a B.S. or M.S. in a scientific discipline or equivalent. The expected work history needed to fill this job is a minimum of three to five years industrial experience in multiple disciplines. The job applicant must have previous know-how in overseeing projects.

A technical services manager is someone at the master's level who is aware of techniques but not necessarily good at the laboratory workbench. This person is capable of answering questions on the telephone.

There are other job titles in biotechnology outside the realm of research. A brief description of some of these follows.

Quality Control Workers

Those involved in quality control usually can be found working at companies that manufacture pharmaceuticals using recombinant DNA procedures or conventional biochemical methods. These drugs are packaged in a sterile fashion. There has to be scrupulous attention paid to cleanliness in the environment where actual bottles are handled.

For instance, quality control inspectors are "on guard" where interferon is made. Little bottles containing the drug roll down a conveyor belt. There has to be constant surveillance of the line. Even the slightest pinholes in any of the bottles could lead to insterility. Quality control personnel rely on equipment to test the integrity of the bottles.

Clinical Researchers

The pharmaceutical industry also is home for the majority of biotechnologists involved in clinical research. Firms start negotiating with the U.S. Food and Drug Administration (FDA) as soon as new drugs are "born" in research and development departments. The FDA mandates a prescribed series of tests to be run by private industry and reviewed by the governmental agency. The process can last for about ten years before FDA grants permission for the drugs to be sold in the United States. Clinical research specialists in industry are devoted to developing, administrating, and analyzing the results of these clinical trials.

Regulatory Affairs

The existence of entities like the U.S. Food and Drug Administration and the Environmental Protection Agency (EPA) has fostered the need for biotechnologists trained in the area of regulatory affairs. The industry needs a whole series of people ranging from lawyers to scientists whose job it is to understand what the governmental regulations are, all the hurdles that will have to be passed, and how that is to be accomplished.

Government employs biotechnologists, too. They are responsible for communicating the government's positions to industry, setting testing standards, and generally making sure that things are done properly.

Manufacturing

The next step after governmental approval of drugs or other biotechnological products is what is known in the industry as scale-up—turning something that was created in small quantities into what now will be a mass-produced item. Biotechnologists are needed to fill a variety of roles in the manufacturing/production sector. Manufacturing personnel commonly have a degree and/or work experience in engineering.

Marketing and Sales

As the biotechnology industry passes from research and development into manufacturing and production, marketing and sales forces will greatly expand, too. Industry needs informed people to act as liaisons between strictly sales personnel and scientists. A Wall Street mentality is sufficient in most marketing situations in the business world, but not in the field of biotechnology. Companies involved in this new science are not addressing laypeople. They are approaching other scientific professionals. Therefore, it is crucial for sales personnel to properly relay the technical benefits of products to customers who need and appreciate such data.

For example, could a scientifically untrained salesperson properly promote human insulin made by recombinant DNA methods rather than from the traditional extraction of insulin from pigs? Physicians want to know how the former is better than the latter. They are interested in how patients react to human insulin versus how they react to insulin made the old-fashioned way.

It is useful to know the broad range of activities that today's biotechnologists can pursue. Most of the current action in the field still takes place in the research laboratories. Because most of the present job opportunities are in research, the following is a description of some of the day-to-day tasks in a laboratory.

DAILY ACTIVITIES IN THE LAB

Plan on putting in a full day's work daily no matter what your job title is. When, for example, a lab assistant enters the laboratory in the morning, he or she takes off the simple gels he or she prepared the preceding day. The lab assistant will photograph them and see what the analysis is. He or she will ask for work assignments from a postdoctoral scientist, scientist I, or research associate. This could involve continuing to process tissue culture cells or bacteria or making DNA from bacteria cultures. This involves spinning the cultures down and making simple manipulations to isolate DNA from the cells. By the end of the day, he or she could be doing some simple digestions of DNA and might also be starting the gels for the next day.

The first thing research associates do when they check into work at the start of the day is to determine what the lab assistants are doing and what jobs should be assigned to them. Research associates might be putting a library of clones (a set of cloned DNA fragments) down onto filters and transferring them with the help of lab assistants.

The postdoctoral research scientist does bench work in the laboratory and also computer work and analysis and writes papers.

As a rule of thumb, the higher the level a person attains in biotechnology, the less time he or she will spend at the lab workbench and the more time that person will spend doing what administrators do.

An outline of the biotechnology job title ladder is comparable to a road map. Both show the routes to get from point A to point B, but neither indicates the speed at which you will complete your trip. In fact, you may not even want to go all the way to point B.

There are some biotechnologists who clearly want to move upward. At the lower levels of the industry, this frequently means earning academic degrees. Many firms actually pay for this education. Some individuals have no interest in the more prestigious job titles. They don't want the more severe responsibilities that come with advancement.

Entry-level positions draw persons with bachelor's degrees who may or may not know what to do with themselves professionally. Often, this includes individuals who plan on being accepted to medical schools in one to two years down the road.

JOB CATEGORIES

Companies engaged in biotechnology-related research and development may vary in the positions they offer, the education and experience required for similar positions, and the responsibilities of the staff at particular job levels. The job categories described below are intended to give a general idea of the positions existing within the industry.

Research and Development

Glass washer
Laboratory assistant
Research associate
Greenhouse assistant
Plant breeder

Quality Control

Quality control analyst
Quality control engineer
Health/safety specialist
Quality assurance auditor
Validation engineer
Validation technician

Clinical Research

Clinical data operator
Clinical programmer analyst
Clinical data specialist
Clinical research associate
Animal technician
Technical writer

Regulatory Affairs

Regulatory affairs specialist
Documentation coordinator/processor
Documentation specialist

Information Systems

Library assistant
Programmer analyst

Marketing and Sales

Market research analyst
Sales representative
Customer service representative
Technical services representative

Manufacturing and Production

Process development engineer
Production planner/scheduler
Manufacturing technician
Packaging/distribution handler
Manufacturing associate
Instrument/calibration technician
Process development associate

Administration

Human resources representative
Patent agent
Buyer

CHAPTER 4

NONSCIENTIFIC CAREER POSSIBILITIES

Most of what is being done by biotechnologists takes place within the confines of company or university laboratories. However, the impact of this growing science is potentially so broad, there is a need for many types of professionals who never are found at traditional workbenches.

Support from experts who do not have scientific and engineering skills is vital to the continued flourishing of biotechnology. As with other fields of interest, it takes a variety of disciplines to "keep the wheels turning." The demand will widen for managers, marketing personnel, salespeople, lawyers, individuals adept at regulatory matters, and financial analysts.

These career areas are even newer than the recently recognized science of biotechnology. Therefore, the educational underpinnings that prepare people for these pursuits are also in their infancy. There will be more development of specific curricula and courses as the need for them increases.

Find out more about some of these employment opportunities by reading the answers to questions posed to several qualified professionals. Their responses are backed by experience in their biotechnological specializations, and you will gain insight into what these job categories are and how you can qualify for them.

PUBLIC RELATIONS

Vice President in a Public Relations Firm Dealing with Biotechnology

Q. Is there a need to let the public know what biotechnology is doing?

A. Certainly. Biotechnology is a field about which most people are not well informed. Some, in fact, are somewhat fearful of it. There are some opponents who are not in favor of the technology and who try to trade on the fears of the public.

Q. Specifically, what type of fears are we concerned with here?

A. Oh, that somehow, in the business of genetic engineering or engineering genes from one species into another species, some awful accident will happen, and some monster will be created or something will be let loose into the environment that won't be able to be placed under control.

Then, down the road, people speculate about human gene therapy and hypothesize about *Brave New World*—sort of alterations of the human species. The fact is that the industry is extremely heavily regulated by the government and also by the NIH and the scientific community itself. There are all kinds of guidelines for what kind of research should and should not be done, so there really isn't anything about which to be concerned. But, there is that group of people that has a lack of understanding. I think many of the products of biotechnology will end up with medical therapeutics or agriculture.

Q. Will you elaborate about how we will benefit from biotechnology?

A. Well, I think the end result of agricultural biotechnology is foods of better quality, foods that, perhaps, are cheaper, because they are easier to produce; foods that are easier to process; foods that will store on the shelf better; and even foods that are improved. There's research, for example, going on in increasing the protein content in everything from potatoes to some of the Third World subsistence crops like cassava, sorghum, and things like that. All this means is that the food is being altered in some minor way. I mean, a potato will still be a potato, but it's reasonable to assume that the public is going to want to know and to be assured that nothing fundamental has been changed about the food being consumed.

Even if some minor genetic alteration were made, it will prompt a need for a tremendous amount of education. People are essentially conservative and take a while to get used to new things. There's a big need for communication.

Q. On that point, has enough been done? Where are we on a spectrum of one to ten in terms of communicating to the public?

A. This technology is different from others in that the industry that's involved in it, the companies that are involved in it, have, from the first, been quite open. For example, there is a difference between what happened during the chemical revolution of the fifties and now. Then we saw the development of new pesticides, weed and insect killers, and all that. There was practically no public communication on that. Companies were just going to make the product, sell it, and move on to another product.

For ten to fifteen years, almost since the technology was developed, there's been a lot of public discussion. Most of the companies involved in it, particularly the small, entrepreneurial ones, put a lot of effort into public communication. They recognize that the government has to understand biotechnology in order to permit research to proceed. The public has to understand it. The users, like farmers, have to understand it. So, there has been increasing communication, but that's not to say that there's been enough.

Q. Would you say the first priority is to get the public involved, then government? Because government is really just an arm of the public.

A. That's true. But, of course, the government regulates it, and, I mean, the regulators regulate, and Congress regulates the regulators....

Q. And the public regulates the Congress.

A. The public tells the Congress what to think and what to do. It's all part of the spectrum.

Q. Do biotechnology firms have internal PR departments, or do they all use outside agencies?

A. Either way. They work through their own people or through their outside consulting agencies.

Q. Are there many public relations agencies that are involved with biotechnology?

A. No. There are some small specialty agencies that you'll find here and there. Some of the larger firms have been tempted to establish biotechnology groups with varying degrees of success. I would say that, by far, we have the largest biotechnology group. We have twenty people in the firm devoted solely to biotechnology communications. The problem, of course, is that with the exception of the large firms, most of the companies are small, start-up, research-oriented firms with no products yet to sell. Therefore, they have no income. They are using venture capital and they are earmarking the proceeds from stock offerings to fund their research. They don't have a lot of money left over to devote to public education.

Q. Do you believe that public relations is crucial to the existence of biotechnology?

A. Oh, I don't think there's any question about it. It could be internal, you know, a company's own PR shop, or the firm could go to an agency. There isn't any question about the need to demystify, if you will, this technology and to reveal it for what it is. It is really a pretty routine, straight-line continuation of classical genetics, that is, crop breeding and animal breeding. It should be made clear that there's nothing new and dramatic and dangerous here. The government has said that, every responsible scientist you can find says there's no unique hazards present here, but somebody has to put that word out.

Q. If it isn't put out, what happens?

A. Then people will shy away from the products. It leaves the field open to those people who are afraid of anything that's new. Also, it leaves the field open to the scaremongers.

Q. How does someone go about getting into the field of public relations in biotechnology?

A. I think that it would be necessary and certainly useful to have some background in science or some degree of comfort, at least, with science and technology. This is a technology that's fairly intricate. It features a lot of big words and a lot of jargon. You have to have some basis in science, which you can learn by coming in at an entry level. We have people here, entry-level employees, who didn't know biotechnology from football when they came in and have learned it from the ground up. But, the main line here is have a background in the sciences. I'm a former science writer. Others here have worked for companies in the field in their internal PR departments.

Q. Are you saying, then, that you, as an employer, would look for a man or woman with a degree in science?

A. No, it doesn't really have to be a degree in science. But, I would say having taken some courses in science would be advisable. We look for someone who knows biology. Biotechnology is basically a biological science. A job candidate should show some experience working with a firm that is somehow involved with medical research or agricultural research or biotechnology research. That certainly helps. However, all this can be learned.

Q. How strongly do you look for someone with a journalistic background?

A. That kind of work history is really not necessary. I'm the only one in our division with any journalistic background. There's a larger consideration, I think. Probably the greatest weakness in the public relations industry and maybe the greatest weakness in our society as a whole is the lack of the ability to write. There are not that many people who learn how to write. I guess it's just a lost art. It's not taught. So somewhere you have to have learned how to write or at least have the ability to learn how to write. Journalism is, obviously, a fine training ground, but the ability to communicate depends heavily on your ability to put down ten sentences that are coherent and track one to the other.

Q. What could a public relations specialist in biotechnology expect to earn? What type of broad range of income is involved?

A. Public relations is a well-paying field. I think by and large it pays better than journalism. Someone with a good deal of experience can earn six figures without too much difficulty.

Q. Are the clients willing to pay, since they are very conscious of the need for public relations?

A. They are willing, but it's more a function of ability because, as I said, most of the good science and good technology is coming out of the small firms, which do not yet have products. They're burning up all their money in research. We represent a number of them. They've got to make sure that their funds last long enough to get the product to the marketplace. They just simply can't afford major public relations activity. I think a breakthrough is coming with the larger companies. Others will start doing what larger companies are doing. So I would say that public relations funding is going to loosen up as the big companies decide that it's something that needs to be done in advance of marketing products. Building a climate of public acceptance is as much a part of the business picture as are research and development.

SALES

Product Development Manager
for a Large Chemical Company

Q. What should a person do to prepare for a sales career in biotechnology? Should one take marketing courses along with those in biotechnology, or should one emphasize marketing in school and learn biotechnology on the job?

A. I'm not sure I can tell you which way would be better. This would vary depending upon which part of the industry one was entering. In either case, it would be good to not necessarily have a thorough technical knowledge, but a good working one to be able to make customers comfortable with the technology.

Remember there's a certain apprehension on the part of the public. People don't understand biotechnology. Many believe the false image of the industry that is spread by some. To make biotechnology successful commercially, we in the industry will have to help people be at ease with it. This partially is the job of salespeople, who must be able to converse in a credible fashion with clientele.

Q. What potential income awaits a marketing specialist in the biotechnology field?

A. I'm probably not the best person to be able to tell you that. I'm in the part of an industry that has geared itself to the chemical and chemical pesticide business. I make no more in my area than my counterparts in other parts of the industry.

When you look at the smaller, venture capital companies in biotechnology, you'll find a higher degree of risk associated with their jobs, because the survival of the firms is often not secure. Because of this, they pay biotechnologists, especially experienced ones, more money than others would get at the more established corporations.

As time goes on, the sky could be the limit in terms of potential income from sales in biotechnology. Here, there isn't the same heavy competition that earmarks marketing in other, long-time industries.

TEACHING

University Biotechnology Professor

Q. What is the state of biotechnology in schools right now?

A. Well, most of the time sciences start in university centers and often trickle down to precollege areas before they become an industrial science. In the area of biotechnology, because of its great potential in a variety of areas, the transition from academia to industry was very rapid. I think that's, perhaps, a sign of our times. The net result, of course, is we frankly do not have enough sufficiently trained people, not only at the technician level, but at the Ph.D. level. For sure, we do not have enough teachers who are trained to teach in this area.

Q. If a person were planning a career in biotechnology and wanted to teach it, what would be the best route to take?

A. I think a person should follow the same path that trains a biology or chemistry teacher. I don't want to get into a debate whether you should get a B.S. in biology and then add an education degree or start as a science educator and get advanced courses in biology or chemistry. This has been argued for decades and will continue to be. I should point out that two of my degrees are in science education and two are in science, so I know both sides of the fence.

But whatever path one would take to end up being a biology or chemistry teacher, one would continue to supplement his or her education through courses in immunology, molecular biology, and so on. The term *biotechnology* is an umbrella. It's almost like saying modern life sciences from my point of view. I don't think it's necessary to go in and take biotechnology I and II. They may not even exist. But if you've taken molecular biology I and II and immunology I and II and fermentation I and II and separation technology I and II and biochemistry I and II, you're very versatile in biotechnology.

The inclination would be for present and potential teachers, as they're developing their biology or chemistry educational backgrounds, to proceed and take as many basic science courses in the areas as possible.

Q. Do you recommend any professional/commercial experience before you go to the classroom?

A. I happen to think that someone who is a teacher already would benefit vastly by taking a course, obviously, like the one I run in the summer, as opposed to going and trying to pretend to be a scientist in a matter of eight weeks. I know there are programs around the country that believe just the opposite, and I respect them. I think there should be room for honest people with different opinions.

But let me give you my rationale. If somebody walks into a lab, be it commercial or academic, with no experience, he or she won't get educated in a matter of eight weeks, unless the lab is ready to shut down and give that person an unbalanced amount of time. Frankly, most biotechnology labs are under a lot of pressure to produce, and they do not have the time to do that. So if what I'm saying is true, the person will end up doing one, two, or three skills, often under the guidance of someone who is relatively junior in the laboratory. The novice, therefore, will not get the vast theoretical background that he or she needs. But to me, the single most important thing that a teacher does is teach. I view the teacher as the conduit of knowledge to the student.

In order to facilitate that, our thought was to take the four weeks and build into them those aspects that we know will work in the classroom. The teacher in the fall can then already be reproducing what he or she learned in the summer.

In the four weeks of our instruction, we structure a core of about twelve or thirteen experiments. By the time our students are through with the four weeks, they have a good command of the theory and practice of these twelve or thirteen experiments.

Q. What's the prognosis in terms of money to be earned?

A. I think we know, unfortunately, in the United States very few precollege or college teachers are rich as a result of their activities in education.

I suppose if one has a good command of biotechnology, he or she may get some recognition in the community that a teacher should really deserve. I think the individual will probably be a centerpiece at the PTA, where he or she will be talking about genetic mutations or how the experiment that you demonstrated to your class or at the PTA can be a diagnostic procedure. I think there's more glory than money involved here.

The important thing is what teachers take to the classroom and how many of our youngsters are going to get excited because of them and go into biotechnology.

Q. Do you foresee more school systems and/or universities picking up on the need to teach biotechnology?

A. Yes. My department, until recently, was biochemistry. It is called biochemistry and molecular biology, because the four new faculty members are practicing certain aspects of biotechnology. The position in industry and academia, by definition, has to grow. Any department in a university or small college that is a biochemistry department or microbiology department or anatomy department is really a basic science department. The biology departments and chemistry departments invariably will have representation from different aspects of biotechnology.

Q. And what about on the secondary level?

A. Two things I think are very important when one talks about educating teachers. I'd like to go back to your question about putting a teacher in a lab in industry. Industry would, I think, serve education much better if it were to financially help programs that gear toward education. We should not rape the educational system. Chances are the best teachers will end up in industry. It would be a shame if our best teachers left classrooms for the higher pay of business.

PATENT LAW

Attorney Who Handles Biotechnology Cases

Q. Do you specialize in biotechnology?

A. We tend to, but we're not limited to that. It's certainly where we have expertise.

Q. Did you take any specific courses in school that would direct you into the biotechnology field?

A. Yes. I started out in science. I had a Ph.D. in biochemistry, and I was an academic researcher running a lab in a university for a number of years before I even contemplated law school. So I came into the field from out of science into law.

Q. Is that the normal way one would approach the subject?

A. There are so few people in this particular area that there's no set route. My personal belief is that the people who do best in the field are people who have advanced degrees in the technology, because its cutting edge is complex. People who come out, even with an undergraduate degree in science, are a little bit behind when it comes to dealing with the scientists who are doing the work. You've got to be able to understand them in order to do good patent work.

Q. Do you consider yourself a lawyer first and a scientist second or equal in both areas?

A. I'm really more of a lawyer now. It's close to equal. I try to go to both kinds of meetings. I go to scientific meetings to keep abreast of the developments in science, and I go to legal meetings to stay abreast with what's happening in the legal area. I do both.

Q. What would be your job description? How do you describe what you do? Do people approach you?

A. Some do. That's usually what happens, because they know what services we have to offer. They approach us with their needs to patent inventions, and that could be persons anywhere from existing corporations to new start-ups. Usually we talk directly to the scientist or the inventor. Less frequently, we deal with something written that they've already produced or some combination of those things.

Q. Is it important for you to speak the scientific language when you fill out papers for the patent office? Do you have to be very scientifically specific?

A. The patent applications should be written in terms that make sense to the scientific community, those who judge them, and other laypeople who may be called upon to read and understand them as well.

Q. So you have to be able to "translate" scientific terminology into layperson's language.

A. Yes. What we're really doing is translating from a scientific context into a patent context. It's not simplifying or popularizing, particularly, but it's different from technical writing in the sense that you're kind of bearing two different audiences in mind at the same time. There'll be a section of the patent that describes in general terms what it's about and what its significance is. Also, there will be a section that is really written for the scientist and a description of what it is. This looks very much like the materials and method section of a scientific paper.

Q. You alluded before to the fact that there are very few of your kind around. Are you in a wide open field?

A. I would say so. As far as I can tell, there's a demand. A few years ago, there used to be a call for people who could hold themselves out to having any knowledge about biology. I would say the demand is not quite that urgent now, but I would say there's still a demand for well-qualified people. This is especially true in corporate patent departments.

Q. Do you envision law schools introducing specific courses in this area, or will one still have to be somewhat dually oriented in terms of biotechnology/patent law education?

A. I think one will have to be dually oriented. I would like to see a time when law schools would sort of take on the job of dealing with law-science related issues in a broad context. There are actually very few law schools that have patent courses.

Q. In other words, the patent field itself is somewhat sparse in terms of personnel?

A. Yes. It's really pretty specialized and you have to point toward it and either go to one of those schools where they teach a number of courses, or you have to make an effort to pick it up outside of your regular law school curriculum.

CHAPTER 5

EDUCATIONAL PREPARATION

Biotechnology is a diverse field. As a result, there is no single recommended way to prepare for a career in this area. The educational routes to a career in biotechnology are as varied as its scope. However, there is a growing roster of programs specifically geared to training biotechnologists. Universities and schools with respected courses in the related sciences also offer alternative approaches to acquiring biotechnological knowledge.

It would be helpful to examine what the campuses of the United States and Canada are doing to meet the personnel needs of biotechnology. Keep in mind this educational menu is subject to change as new classes are added to school catalogs. You also might want to talk to representatives of firms in the field to ascertain what training they prefer their potential employees to have.

Many academics and industry observers believe that the best preparation for biotechnology is training in a traditional discipline, such as genetics or plant physiology, while learning some of the tools of biotechnology. Individuals with such backgrounds then can work on interdisciplinary teams and focus on specific problems for which they are best qualified.

David Pramer, former director of the Waksman Institute of Microbiology at Rutgers University, commented:

> It would be unwise for universities to offer educational programs in biotechnology that are narrowly conceived or overly professional, and it is essential for university scientists within traditional academic disciplines not to abdicate a responsibility to educate biotechnologists....
>
> To continue to flourish, biotechnology must be nourished by a steady supply of individuals who also are well educated in traditional disciplines.... Since biotechnology five years from now may be quite different from what it is today, the key to educating a biotechnologist is flexibility in specialized aspects of a program that is firmly based in science and engineering.

Because of the broad range of applications in this field, biotechnology firms require a diversity of scientific skills. A solid background in the life sciences is necessary for virtually all positions. The disciplines most in demand include the following:

Agricultural sciences
Biochemical engineering
Biochemistry
Biology
Botany

Chemistry
Computer science
Enzymology
Genetics
Immunology
Microbiology
Molecular biology
Mycology
Veterinary medicine
Virology
Zoology

NEW STEPS IN BIOTECHNOLOGY EDUCATION

In recent years, training and education provided by colleges and universities has been expanded to keep up with the educational and research demands of the emerging biotechnology industry. Available programs include two-year (associate) degree programs, four-year degree programs, graduate degree programs, and short courses in particular biotechnologies designed for professional scientists. Also important are university-based biotechnology research centers. While these centers generally do not sponsor courses or grant degrees, they do enhance biotechnology education on their campuses. They offer access to equipment, faculty development, and research opportunities for both graduates and undergraduates. These centers also provide a focal point for discussions of how best to educate and train new biotechnologists.

For the most part, university programs have been developed with little or no coordination among the program developers at different schools. Most do, however, have some form of interaction with industry. These contacts with industry include surveying local biotechnology companies and sending program proposals to them for comments.

Age of Programs

With the exception of programs in biochemical engineering, most biotechnology programs are relatively new. The oldest began in 1980. Many more were developed or expanded in the 1980s and 1990s.

A large number of biotechnology programs were set up in 1983. This indicates a two-year lag from 1981, the year many of the first biotechnology companies were founded. Two years is a relatively short time in which to develop curricula and approve programs. Some institutions moved quickly into biotechnology at that time. Other programs were formed later in the 1980s and the 1990s.

There is no clear pattern of which degree-level programs were founded first. In each year, a mix of them started. They were aimed at a variety of educational levels. Community college programs are usually newer than bachelor's and master's programs.

At the doctoral level, most programs are in bioprocessing or biochemical engineering. One exception is the Iowa Biotechnology Training Program's Ph.D. in microbiology and immunology. Traditional Ph.D. programs in molecular biology, microbiology, biochemistry, and other fields also support the biotechnology industry.

Program Curricula

Recombinant DNA techniques initially formed the core of many of the programs developed first. Courses or skills commonly taught include tissue culturing, hybridoma technology, immunochemistry, bioprocess engineering, fermentation, and purification and separation sciences.

The extent to which training in bioprocess engineering is available is not clear. Only a few programs have in-depth faculty expertise; most expertise is scattered among chemical engineering departments.

The vast majority of the undergraduate chemical engineering curriculum is mandated by the accreditation standards of the American Institute of Chemical Engineers and the Accreditation Board for Engineering and Technology. In some universities, students interested in biochemical engineering are urged to use their limited electives for courses in biochemistry, microbiology, biochemical engineering, genetics, and biology.

Training programs tend to be laboratory intensive, except for short courses and workshops. Academic program directors who have contacted industry representatives about their needs have routinely found that industry requires technicians with hands-on laboratory experience, and they have designed their programs accordingly.

ASSOCIATE DEGREE PROGRAMS

The need for biotechnicians with specialized, but limited, training has prompted a number of community colleges to institute or consider instituting biotechnology training programs. Early in the development of biotechnology, most work was done by highly educated, innovative thinkers, who often had to develop new procedures as their research progressed. As with all technologies, as biotechnology matured, more of the work has become routine and can be assigned to less highly trained technicians, for whom a two-year training program may be very appropriate.

A number of associate of applied sciences (AAS) programs in biotechnology are taught at community or junior colleges or at state colleges. These programs are designed to fill the need for biotechnicians (similar to the more established need of chemical technicians), although students from these programs may go on to four-year colleges.

The need for biotechnicians at the AAS level has increased in recent years, but a huge need for personnel trained at this level has not yet emerged. Among the factors influencing the development of associate degree programs in biotechnology are the following:

- Training demands for technicians in biotechnology differ from current technicians in other technology fields, most significantly in that they require a broader and more interdisciplinary technical base.
- Many biotechnology companies prefer biotechnicians to have at least a bachelor's degree.
- The biotechnology industry's present need for employment of biotechnicians from two-year training programs is not large enough to justify the expense of starting new programs at many two-year institutions.
- Two-year programs hold more potential in areas with the largest markets for biotechnicians, including California, Massachusetts, New Jersey, New York, and Maryland. The need for biotechnicians exists in other parts of the country and will expand in some states.

Some industry officials have not been supportive of the two-year programs thus far. Concerns have included whether two years in college can provide the knowledge necessary to manage complex instrumentation and sensitive organisms, and that technicians without a theoretical understanding may not be able to adapt to the ever-changing needs of a rapidly evolving technology.

Industry representatives have also given these reasons for skepticism: at times there has been an oversupply of B.S.- and M.S.-degreed biologists available for technician work;

two-year programs lack the breadth and depth of four-year programs; and companies need the research background provided by B.S. and M.S. programs.

Some reasons for reluctance in hiring graduates of two-year programs has dissipated as dedicated biotechnology companies grow and mature. For example, small companies are more likely to require their employees to assume multiple duties, some of which will require more training than two-year programs provide. As a company's overall workload and staff increase, it can divide tasks by level of skill and may be able to employ people full-time at the lower skill levels. Also, as work continues to shift from research and development to production, more of the tasks will become routine. Larger companies may also be able to afford more time for on-the-job training.

Following is an overview of several programs offered at the two-year level.

Madison Area Technical College

A good example of a technician-level program is the Biotechnology Laboratory Technician Program offered by Madison Area Technical College in Wisconsin. This two-year course of study leads to an associate degree. It prepares students to work in laboratories, typically in research and development laboratories or small-scale production facilities. Students acquire skills and knowledge in such areas as documentation, instrumentation, chromatography, microbiology, fermentation, protein purification methods, and recombinant DNA methodologies.

Prerequisites for admission to this program include an interest in science; previous completion of high school classes in biology, chemistry, and algebra (or the equivalent); and completion of a high school diploma or GED.

Students learn skills such as fermentation technology, cell culturing, and protein purification. Their experience includes serving as an intern in a local laboratory.

The four-semester associate program includes thirty-seven credits of program courses, twelve credits of science support courses, fifteen credits of general education courses, and six credits of elective courses. Examples of program courses include:

Instrumentation and Introduction to Basic Laboratory Methods
Chromatography Techniques

For more information contact:

Biotechnology Program
  Madison Area Technical College
  3550 Anderson Street
  Madison, WI 53704

Foothill College

Foothill College in Los Altos, California, offers a two-year biotechnology program. Many students enroll in the full-time program, while others participate in evening short-course offerings to obtain hands-on experience. Students use these skills to obtain jobs in laboratories, research, product development, manufacturing, quality control, and clinical studies.

Students may choose from two basic program options. A one-year sequence of courses leads to a certificate of proficiency in biotechnology. This program prepares students to compete for technician-level jobs in laboratories and biotechnology firms or with other employers.

A two-year expanded program leads to an associate degree in biotechnology and offers graduates the option of transferring to a four-year college or entering the job market with additional training.

Course offerings in the certificate program include:

Fundamental Biological Concepts I, II, and III
Principles of Library Research
Laboratory Safety
Plant Biotechnology: Micropropagation
Microbiology
Survey of Organic and Biochemistry
Using the Computer
Biotechnology Externship
Laboratory Animal Care Course

Students completing an Associate in Science Degree complete a number of other courses including general education requirements, elective biotechnology courses, a course in cell biology, and a statistics course.

For more program details contact:

Foothill College
12345 El Monte Road
Los Altos, CA 94022-4599

Montgomery College

Another technician-level program is the Biotechnology Laboratory Technician program offered by Maryland's Montgomery College. This associate degree program prepares students to work as skilled technicians under the supervision of research scientists in the biological, chemical, and physical sciences.

Students learn a variety of laboratory skills and complete basic courses in mathematics, biology, and chemistry as well as more specialized courses.

A typical sequence of courses followed by full-time students is as follows:

First Semester:
  Principles of Biology
  Introduction to the Laboratory
  Principles of Chemistry I
  Techniques of Reading and Writing
  Mathematics Foundation

Second Semester:
  Microbiology
  Cell Function and Morphology
  Principles of Chemistry II
  English Foundation

Summer Session:
  Computer Applications I
  Health Foundation
  Speech Foundation

Third Semester:
  General Genetics
  Biotechnology I—Nucleic Acid Analysis
  Essentials of Organic and Biochemistry
  Chemistry Elective

Fourth Semester:
  Immunology
  Biotechnology Practicum I
  Biotechnology II—Protein and Cell Techniques
  Arts or Humanities Distribution
  Behavioral and Social Sciences Distribution

Summer Session:
  Biotechnology Practicum II
  Biotechnology Practicum III

Information about admission and other matters is available by contacting:

Biotechnology Laboratory Technician Program
Montgomery College
51 Mannakee Street
Rockville, MD 20850

BACHELOR'S- AND GRADUATE-LEVEL PROGRAMS

Numerous colleges and universities have instituted bachelor's-level programs in biotechnology. Like the two-year programs, these programs emphasize hands-on laboratory experience but include more theoretical science and humanities courses. Students are prepared either to go directly to work in industrial labs or to enter master's or doctoral programs. Several examples of such programs are described below.

University of Wisconsin-River Falls

This program represents an interdepartmental program emphasizing the molecular basis of life processes and the techniques utilized to study and control these processes. Students take an integrated sequence of courses selected from the curricula of the departments of biology, chemistry, physics, animal and food sciences, and plant and earth sciences.

Participating students pursue a B.S. degree in biotechnology in either the College of Arts and Sciences or Agriculture.

A typical four-year plan of study pursued through the College of Arts and Sciences would be as follows (with some variance from student to student):

YEAR 1

Fall

General Chemistry I
General Chemistry Lab I
Introduction to Biology
Freshman English I
Calculus
Physical Education—Lifetime Activities

Spring

General Chemistry II
General Chemistry Lab II
Freshman English II
General Education—Social and Behavioral Sciences
General Education—Fine Arts
Health and Fitness for Life

YEAR 2

Fall

Organic Chemistry I
Organic Chemistry Lab I
General Botany or General Zoology
General Physics

General Physics Lab
Modern Language

Spring
Organic Chemistry II
Organic Chemistry Lab II
Cell Biology
General Physics
General Physics Lab
General Education—Literature
Physical Education—Lifetime Activities

YEAR 3

Fall
Analytical Chemistry
Analytical Chemistry Lab
Biochemistry I
Bacteriology
General Education—Social and Behavioral Sciences

Spring
Biochemistry II
Biochemistry Lab
Plant Tissue Culture: Theory and Practice
Genetics and Evolution
Animal Cell Culture
Biotech Elective

YEAR 4

Fall

Biotech Elective
Food Microbiology
Molecular Biology
Virology
Bioethics

Spring

Biotech Elective
Biotechnology Seminar
Interdisciplinary Capstone—Humanities
Interdisciplinary Capstone—Social Science
General Education—Liberal Arts (Cultural Diversity)
General Elective

For more details contact:

Biotechnology Program
University of Wisconsin-River Falls
410 South Third Street
River Falls, WI 54022

Georgia Tech

At Georgia Institute of Technology (Georgia Tech) in Atlanta, students who pursue a bachelor's degree in biology may choose a biotechnology track from among three specialty tracks. Along with a full slate of courses required for biology majors, they complete twenty-one to twenty-two credits hours in the following areas of microbial biotechnology and microbiology:

Medical Bacteriology
Microbial Genetics
Microbial Genetics Lab
Microbial Physiology
Microbial Physiology Lab
Microbial Ecology
Industrial Microbiology
Fermentation Lab

For more information contact:

School of Biology
Georgia Institute of Technology
Atlanta, GA 30332-0230

University of Missouri-St. Louis

The Department of Biology at this university offers an undergraduate certificate in biotechnology as part of its B.A. and B.S. degree in biology, along with a similar certificate as part of its M.S. and Ph.D. degrees in biology.

At the bachelor's degree level, students may obtain an undergraduate certificate in biotechnology by completing specified courses along with those required for the bachelor's degree including all science course requirements of the B.S. in biology program.

Biotechnology courses (some of which are required for the certificate and some of which are optional) include:

Microbiology
Microbiology Laboratory
Genetics Laboratory
Biological Chemistry Laboratory
Introduction to Biotechnology
Gene Expression in Eukaryotes
Gene Expression in Prokaryotes
Immunobiology
Techniques in Molecular Biology
Molecular Cell Biology
Virology
Topics in Biological Chemistry
Advanced Biochemistry

The graduate certificate can be earned independently or in conjunction with a master's or doctoral degree in biology. It consists of an eighteen-credit-hour program including courses in the following areas:

Techniques in Molecular Biology
Gene Expression in Eukaryotes
Gene Expression in Prokaryotes
Elective courses in Immunology, Cell Biology, and Biochemistry

An internship program is also available. For more information contact:

Department of Biology
  University of Missouri-St. Louis
  R223 Research Building
  8001 Natural Bridge Road
  St. Louis, MO 63121

Master's degree programs in biotechnology are multidisciplinary and often interdepartmental. Many programs preparing students for careers in bioprocessing are at the master's and doctoral levels, since most people in the industry consider M.S. and Ph.D. degrees to be entry-level requirements for bioprocessing jobs.

Doctoral degrees are considered the most desirable and are required for the most advanced positions. Following is an overview of several programs offered at the graduate level.

McGill University

Canada's McGill University offers a short-term Graduate Certificate in Biotechnology. This program is designed for students who already hold a four-year degree in the biological or medical sciences, providing additional backgroundto help students prepare for jobs in the biotechnology industry.

The program may be completed in four months. During this time, students gain hands-on laboratory experience based on the latest molecular biology techniques. They may also benefit from a biotechnology management course, which provides information on how the biotechnology industry works, and some students participate in a twelve-week practicum involving placement in a biotechnology company.

The program consists of three required courses and two complementary courses totaling fifteen credit hours. For more information contact:

Graduate Certificate in Biotechnology
  Macdonald Campus, McGill University
  Lakeshore Road, Ste. Anne de Bellevue
  Montreal, Quebec
  Canada H9X 3V9

University of Pennsylvania

The University of Pennsylvania offers a Master of Biotechnology Program with a cross-disciplinary approach. Students prepare for careers in the biotechnology and pharmaceutical industries. Students choose from three program tracks:

1. Basic Biotechnology (emphasizing basic molecular biology)
2. Engineering Biotechnology (stressing bioprocess engineering central to pharmaceutical manufacturing)
3. Computational Biology/Bioinformatics (preparing students for analysis of expanding genomic databases)

Students enrolling in this program complete eleven computational courses consisting of six core courses and five courses from the chosen track. Core curriculum courses in the Basic Biotechnology track include the following:

Biochemistry

Biotechnology I, a course covering molecular biology, recombinant DNA technology, transgenic organisms, protein engineering, combinatorial chemistry, and molecular modeling

Biotechnology II: Engineering Biotechnology, covering production of biological molecules using cell culture technologies. This course includes an introduction to bioreactor design and control, molecular and cellular bioseparations, and tissue and cellular engineering

Laboratory in Biotechnology and Genetic Engineering

Statistics

Biotechnology Seminar I and II, providing an overview of current scientific, regulatory, and ethical issues in biotechnology. Topics include drug discovery, elements of pharmaceutical patent law, design of clinical trials, FDA approval process, developments in computational biology, practical aspects of clinical pharmacology, and contemporary issues in bioethics

Other courses in this track include:

Molecular Genetics

Experimental Principles in Molecular Biology

Advanced Cell Biology

Advanced Developmental Biology

Genetic Systems

Immunobiology

Prokaryotic Molecular Genetics

Current Topics in Plant Molecular Biology
Mammalian Developmental Biology
Thesis Research (two terms of independent study)

Core courses in the Engineering Biotechnology track include:

Pharmaceutical Manufacturing, a continuation of Biotechnology II covering production of biological molecules, bioreactors, bioseparations, tissue and cellular engineering
Cell Biology and Molecular Structure

Other courses in this track include:

Quantitative Human Physiology
Biomechanics and Transport
Foundations of Engineering Mathematics I
Foundations of Engineering Mathematics II
Interfacial Bioscience
Transport Processes I and II
Biomaterials
Biomedical Instrumentation
Biochemistry
Molecular Biophysics
Molecular Genetics
Computational Biology
Advanced Cell Biology
Cellular Bioengineering
Pharmaceutical Manufacturing

Fundamentals of Pharmacology
Mechanics of Biomaterials

Core courses in the Computational Biology/Bioinformatics track include:

Statistics II
Computational Biology (two courses)

Other courses include:

Programming Languages
Algorithms
Databases
Advanced Databases

For more details contact:

Master of Biotechnology
Towne Building, Room 111
University of Pennsylvania
Philadelphia, PA 19104

University of Texas-Stephen F. Austin University

An interesting program is offered by the University of Texas Health Center at Tyler, Texas, and the Stephen F. Austin State University at Nacogdoches, Texas, who have combined their scientific faculties and research and educational facilities to offer a graduate program in biotechnology.

The program allows students to acquire knowledge and skills in biotechnology along with an academic background in biochemistry. Students who successfully complete the program earn an M.S. degree in biotechnology from Stephen F. Austin State University.

To complete the program, students take eighteen credit hours of required core courses providing background in biochemistry, molecular biology, and the theoretical applications of biotechnology, along with six elective credit hours and twelve research hours including a thesis research project.

An innovative angle is that core lecture courses use tele-video conferencing equipment, meaning that students can attend classes at either of the participating campuses. They combine this lecture approach with hands-on laboratory experiences in areas such as the following:

Basic Biotech Laboratory Procedures
Molecular Genetics
Gene Manipulation and Modification
Gene Expression
PCR Technology
DNA Sequencing
Protein Biochemistry
Protein Synthesis and Purification
Amino Acid Sequencing
Applications of Immunology
Fermentation Technology

For more information contact:

Biotechnology Graduate Program
　The University of Texas Health Center
　11937 U.S. Highway 271
　Tyler, TX 75708

RESEARCH CENTERS

University-based biotechnology research centers take many forms. Purposes of the centers frequently include conducting or sponsoring research, coordinating biotechnology research and training among the various university departments, providing a forum for multidisciplinary projects, and purchasing specialized equipment. Centers may also be involved with local biotechnology companies in technology transfer and economic development activities. Some centers sponsor short courses in laboratory techniques for both academic and industrial scientists.

In addition to those described earlier, other colleges and research institutes with biotechnology programs include:

Colorado Institute of Research in Biotechnology
　University of Colorado
　Department of Chemical Engineering
　Boulder, CO 80309

University of Illinois Biotechnology Center
　901 South Mathews Avenue
　Urbana, IL 61801

University of Maryland
　College of Life Sciences
　1109 Microbiology Building
　College Park, MD 20742

Virginia Tech
    Fralin Biotechnology Center
    Blacksburg, VA 24061

Northwestern University Center for Biotechnology
    BIRL
    1801 Maple Avenue
    Evanston, IL 60201

Canadian institutions offering biotechnology programs include:

University of British Columbia
    2329 West Mall
    Vancouver, BC
    Canada V6T 1Z4

University of Calgary
    2500 University Drive NW
    Calgary, AB
    Canada T2N 1N4

Dalhousie University
    Halifax, NS
    Canada B3H 3J5

McGill University
    845 Sherbrooke St. W
    Montreal, Quebec
    Canada H3A 2T5

University of Montreal
    Montreal, Quebec
    Canada H3T 1P1

University of Toronto
    Toronto, ON
    Canada M5S 1A1

These are just some of the colleges and universities offering programs in biotechnology. For more information about available programs, contact the state coordinating council for higher education for any state in which you are interested. Or contact schools directly and obtain catalogs of course offerings.

CONTINUING EDUCATION

Continuing education has emerged as a significant need, given the rapid development of new biotechniques and the large number of researchers who received their formal training before new techniques were widely integrated into biological research. Short courses described previously are a principal way of accomplishing this continuing education. In addition, most biotechnology companies provide training funds for their employees.

Continuing education is an integral part of many companies' day-to-day operations. Companies hold seminars, sponsor cross-departmental training, and establish systems to keep their research staffs abreast of current literature.

Continuing education is also a principal motivation for companies to enter into collaborative arrangements with universities. These arrangements frequently allow company scientists to spend time in university laboratories, updating their skills.

CHAPTER 6

EMPLOYMENT OPPORTUNITIES

Employment prospects can be found in biotechnology for recent graduates with degrees ranging from a high school diploma to a Ph.D. There are opening for graduates with a background in science, particularly biology, genetics, molecular biology, biochemistry, microbiology, cell biology, and animal or plant biology. An increasing number of biotechnology positions also are becoming available for chemists and chemical engineers, physicists, engineers, and computer information scientists. As more and more new products such as medicines, agrochemicals, and animal health drugs are created and approved by the FDA, specialists such as doctors, veterinarians, ecologists, pharmacologists, and toxicologists are needed to assess product safety. The expansion of the industry is also creating opportunities for people with training in management, marketing, sales, finance, and information processing.

INDUSTRY FACTS AND TRENDS

Because biotechnology has received extensive coverage in the press, it is easy to forget that the field is actually still in its early stages. In the 1970s biotechnology was barely an industry at all, largely unheard of by most people. By the 1980s, it had grown into a $2-billion market. By the end of the 1990s, biotechnology had grown explosively. In 1998, $97 billion had been invested in the U.S. biotechnology industry.

According to the Biotechnology Industry Organization (BIO), the United States is currently the world leader in biotechnology product research, development, and commercialization. Biotechnology products currently on the market include life-saving health care goods and microbial pesticides. Recent biotechnological advances are soon expected to offer healthier foods, disease- and insect-resistant crops, new energy sources, environmental cleanup techniques, and more.

The industry facts and statistics that follow in this chapter are provided courtesy of the Biotechnology Industry Organization.

Number and Location of U.S. Biotechnology Companies

Currently there are more than 1,280 companies in the United States at work in some area of biotechnology. Certain geographical areas have a high concentration of biotechnology companies, including the following:

San Francisco Bay
New England
Mid-Atlantic
San Diego
New York
Los Angeles/Orange County
Philadelphia/Delaware Valley
New Jersey
Texas
Seattle
North Carolina
Wisconsin
Ohio
Illinois
Iowa

Company Size

The following is breakdown of biotechnology companies by size:

Size	Percentage of Companies
Small (1–50 employees)	37%
Mid-size (51–135 employees)	33%
Large (136–299 employees)	18%
Top tier (300+ employees)	12%

Employment

There are currently more than 150,000 people employed in the biotechnology industry, an increase of almost 50 percent since 1995. Because so many biotechnology companies are small and relatively new, many offer excellent incentive compensation plans in place of high salaries including:

Stock-option plans
401K plans
Companywide stock purchase plans
· Cash-bonus plans

Areas of Product Development

Biotechnology companies are currently developing products in the following industry areas:

Market Segment	Percentage of Companies
Therapeutic	42%
Human diagnostics	26%
Supplier	15%
Chemical, environmental, and services	9%
Agricultural	8%

Research and Development

The money being invested in biotechnology research and development is a good gauge of the industry's potential for growth in 2000 and beyond. Biotechnology companies are currently spending approximately $4.9 billion a year on research and development (R&D). This is a 42 percent increase since 1991.

Sales and Revenues

The total revenue of public and private biotechnology companies is now over $18 billion, more than double the total in 1993. And total product sales now exceed $13 billion.

Export sales of U.S. biotechnology products are growing. Biotechnology companies in the United States are currently selling their products in many parts of the world, including the following:

Canada
Eastern Europe
Russia
Japan
Latin America
Pacific Rim
Western Europe

SALARIES AND BENEFITS

Salaries earned by biotechnology professionals vary widely. In many cases, salaries may be quite good, especially for experienced scientists, technicians, and other personnel.

In general, salaries paid by colleges or other nonprofit employers are not as high as those for comparable positions in private business. Private employers may also offer stock options or other incentives. But regardless of the type of employer, salaries in this field can be quite attractive.

According to the U.S. Department of Labor, biological scientists earned median salaries of $46,140 in 1998. Other salary figures of note include the following, according to the DOL:

- Salaries of the middle 50 percent of those employed ranged from $35,200 to $67,850
- The highest 10 percent earned more than $86,000
- Median annual salaries in the following areas were:
  Federal government $48,600
  Drugs $46,300
  Research and testing services $40,800

In 1999, biological scientists employed by the federal government earned an average salary of $56,000.

Salaries in private industry vary widely. In some cases, scientists in the biotechnology field have become wealthy by starting their own companies or developing patents that have led to lucrative profits.

Salaries for technicians in this field range from about $16,000 to more than $40,000 annually, according to the U.S. Department of Labor. Factors affecting salary levels include:

educational background
skill and experience
geographical location
size and type of employer
level of responsibility
previous or existing salary
competition for employees

Fringe Benefits

Most employers provide a variety of benefits to employees in addition to salaries. These might include some or all of the following:

medical insurance
dental insurance
life insurance
stock options and/or profit sharing
disability insurance
holidays
sick time
personal time
retirement plans
tuition assistance

PERSONNEL NEEDS

Recently the biotechnology industry has shifted much of its emphasis away from basic research, focusing on converting research findings into marketable products. This means that many companies are moving from the research and development phase into production and marketing.

Although there is still a need for research scientists, this industry shift has created an increasing number of job opportunities for production engineers, marketing specialists, human resource specialists, administrative assistants, public relations specialists, data-processing staff, accountants, programmers, and other business specialists.

Many companies, particularly mid-size and large firms, look for managers with a combination of business and technical backgrounds. For example, a person with a B.S. in the biological sciences and an M.B.A., or a person with an undergraduate business degree and a master's degree in environmental policy, would be very useful to companies developing agricultural or veterinary products. The composition of the biotechnological industry directly affects its job seekers.

Quite often, small companies in biotechnology, many of them in the health care field, experience management difficulties and are "swallowed up" by larger corporations. If the consolidation movement continues, the industry's efforts may focus on new areas of biotechnology.

Stay aware of the changing faces of the subindustries that comprise biotechnology. Study the newspaper reports in scientific magazines, journals, and the financial press. Be alert to the latest employment want ads. Your career preparation, based upon your realistic feel for the needs of the field today and tomorrow, will pay off for you.

Personnel shortages in certain emerging fields are largely unavoidable. This is due both to the difficulty of predicting which fields will have the heaviest demands and the lag time required for educational institutions to gear up for new fields. The expense of new faculty and new equipment prevents schools from rapidly moving into them. It frequently follows that in areas where there is a shortage of researchers, there also are not enough university instructors. For example, pharmaceutical companies are "plucking" x-ray crystallographers with skills in working with biological molecules off of campuses at a rate that threatens to undercut both research and the training of future crystallographers.

In another example, a lack of microbial ecologists resulted from increased interest in the release of engineered organisms into the environment. The U.S. Environmental Protection Agency (EPA) pronounced some of the functions of microbial ecologists as priority areas. These areas included ecological risk assessment, ecosystem structure and workings, and ecological and toxicological effects. Until recently, microbial ecology was a relatively obscure field that attracted less money and talent than the more glamorous fields such as molecular biology.

In recent decades, protein chemistry has emerged as a high-need field. The knowledge of making, purifying, and stabilizing proteins to their active form is required, especially in pharmaceutical applications. The need for immunologists has increased, too, due to demand in both monoclonal antibody development and in AIDS research.

Whether shortages of bioprocess engineers actually materialize will depend on how rapidly biotechnology products are brought to the marketplace and how and when universities and their students respond to predicted personnel needs. While a shortage of bioprocess engineers would be "a serious bottleneck" for the industry, the actual number of them that will be needed will not be that great. Bioprocess engineering does not demand a large work force. It has been estimated that personnel requirements for bioprocessing, even after firms enter mass production, will be only 10 to 15 percent of all those employed in biotechnology. Technological advances such as biosensors and computer-controlled continuous bioprocessing could reduce the need for bioprocess engineers.

Potential personnel shortages may also be eased somewhat by scientist mobility. It was thought at one time, for instance, that the supply of plant molecular biologists was running low. In fact, however, the field of plant molecular biology expanded at a rapid pace in more recent years due to the large pool of molecular biology postdoctoral fellows and trainees. While many of these scientists were specialists in animal or bacterial systems, they were able to apply their skills and knowledge of molecular genetics to plant systems. The postdoctoral pool thus served as a buffer, although the need remained for biotechnologists with plant expertise.

No such postdoctoral pool has traditionally existed for bioprocess engineering. A soft market for petrochemical engineers creates a logical pool of possible bioprocess engineers should shortages become acute. The problem is that traditional chemical engineers generally have no understanding of living systems, because they have spent their professional lives working with nonliving varieties.

Universities have responded with some increased attention to bioprocess engineering. Nevertheless, newer biotechnology programs tend to emphasize engineering less than genetic manipulation techniques. College students appear to be highly responsive to the signals of the market. They can be expected to seek out educational programs for all the various aspects of biotechnology that they believe will offer occupational rewards.

Belief is widespread that interdisciplinary training should be increased, but opinions vary with regard to the specific disciplines that should be included. Industrialists have referred to the need for "life-science-oriented engineers and engineering-oriented life scientists" as well as chemical engineers with an appreciation of biosynthesis and biologists with an understanding of production problems.

Different types of firms have different personnel needs. Generally, smaller firms have a higher percentage of Ph.D. scientists than do larger ones. Small firms are more likely to be concentrating on relatively basic research and development. Thus, they have more Ph.D. research scientists. Small firms are also less likely to be involved in large-scale production and can, therefore, be expected to have less need for technicians than their larger counterparts. Some analysts have concluded that small firms are less able to afford on-the-job training. They need people who can get up to speed right away. Other experts find that employers are interested in persons with broad general education. They are willing to teach special skills on the job.

The job openings are there and will continue to mount. Prospective biotechnologists should be advised that their employment advancement opportunities and rewards will build in direct proportion to the educational credentials and work experience they offer their prospective employers.

CHAPTER 7

SUCCEEDING IN BIOTECHNOLOGY

If you can demonstrate a history of textbook learning and solid, on-the-job work performance, you will probably get the attention of a company's hiring specialist. Yet a job quest can be lost for you or any candidate who appears to be lacking other basic ingredients needed for productive participation in biotechnology.

These qualities might be considered as intangibles—hard-to-pinpoint personality traits with which one is born. However, the aptitudes and attitudes that please employers can be acquired and maintained. Know what these behavioral characteristics are, and make them a part of the way you conduct yourself. They do make the difference between a job offer and a job rejection.

This chapter outlines worthwhile ways of thinking and the conduct that biotechnologists should practice. Many are applicable to scientists in all fields. Others are especially unique to a pioneer science that, quite frequently, expects its personnel to be flexible enough to master challenging assignments not yet covered in textbooks.

COMMUNICATING

Biotechnologists must relate to people who may have more or less sophisticated education than they do. The knack of communicating on all levels is crucial.

There may be a tendency to view the wonders of biotechnology from an intellectual perspective, forgetting at times the "down-to-earth" duty of keeping customers of your company happy and informed. Biotechnologists, therefore, should possess the sales abilities to tell clients how products will help them.

Regardless if you are a scientist, executive, or marketing person in a corporate setting, you are always selling your ideas. You are attempting to convince others that your thoughts make sense. The more you enjoy and take pride in your work, the more persuasive you will be. If you can get someone to think of something in the same way you do, even if that individual does not come to your same conclusion, you have accomplished a sales job.

COOPERATING IN THE LAB

In the laboratory, be willing to endure long hours to get a job done. Have the perseverance to attack problems from a variety of angles that may or may not be taught in classrooms.

Realize that when you complete an assignment, you may not necessarily be finished with it. Always look for that additional something that could be done to draw your work to a successful conclusion.

Work as a team player. Do not limit your efforts only to your assigned job. Help others in your research group with their projects.

It is commendable to be able to focus upon a goal that has been set by a research and development group. Be dedicated to the completion of the project you and your scientist peers deemed so important yesterday. But if the priority of the undertaking changes, be able to adjust to keep in tune with your current needs.

Keep in mind that scientists in this field cannot do whatever they feel like doing. They must profess willingness to be controlled by some other person or group of people responsible for making the decisions as to what can be attempted.

If you are comfortable working by yourself to compile research details and then exchanging your findings with others in your company, you will do well in biotechnology. The ideal person in this field is someone who is an "introverted extrovert," who can give birth to theories but gear those ideas to the real world.

MAKING THE MOST OF YOUR EXPERIENCE

Some human resource officers and personnel agencies seek job candidates with B.S. or M.S. degrees who have solid, broad foundations in the hard sciences of chemistry, physics, and mathematics. They believe this background foretells an ability to be versatile on the job. It also indicates learned discipline that will be beneficial to a researcher as he or she moves up the job ladder of biotechnology.

College degrees are proof to employers that those who hold them are willing to be trained. This is important in an industry where on-the-job learning is the rule rather than the exception.

Of course, college diplomas also are evidence of goal setting and fulfillment, regardless of how long it takes. In the workplace, workers who have accomplished this goal are often aggressive self-starters who are able to get their jobs done with little or no close supervision.

Surprisingly, if your resume shows you have worked in a company that has undergone change, you may be of special worth to some hiring officials. Your job record backs up your ability for adjusting to stress, something that might not be so obvious if your work history stated you worked with just one employer for a long period of time.

COPING WITH FRUSTRATIONS

Those who work in the pharmaceutical end of biotechnology admit to a presently unavoidable job frustration. They think they must resign themselves to what they call lengthy waits for new drug approval from the U.S. Food and Drug

Administration. Sometimes, this means that interested employees cannot see a project through from inception to completion unless they are willing to pursue such goals over a period of years.

At the same time, research scientists in all areas of biotechnology live with another type of tension—competition. The competitive nature of this demanding field can contribute to job stress.

Of course, it is human nature for a person to want to make a name for himself or herself in a field that is itself making history. Today's reputation is tomorrow's legend. This motivating force to excel is healthy as long as it is exhibited in a positive manner. Competition among firms in the industry should be welcomed, too. The innovation it fosters is good news for all.

The push for progress should proceed on a high moral plane. If you are a scientist reporting what you are doing, you have to communicate the truth. As with all endeavors, there is always the temptation to enhance the facts. Good scientists record what they see, whether or not it fits into their preconceived theories.

The temptation to "fudge" that some might consider is not unique to biotechnology. However, due to the nature of this embryonic science, its practitioners are vulnerable to wanting to make fast strides. It should be emphasized that intellectual honesty has not been a major problem in biotechnology, and it is not expected to be so in the future by those in the field. There, too, exists the possibility of more and more review boards coming into being to double-check research results.

BEING SENSITIVE TO PUBLIC PERCEPTIONS

Remember, biotechnologists are altering life-forms. Do not ignore an underlying popular fear that monsters might escape out of some laboratory or that some scientists deliberately release genetically engineered organisms into the environment. It is smart to stay in touch with public opinion and be able to answer it as it relates to the ethical considerations of biotechnology. Any science that is manipulating nature must be subject to public scrutiny and control such as legislation and permits.

Polls and surveys have shown that the American people have mixed feelings about biotechnology and its regulation. On the one hand, many feel that the risks of biotechnology have been greatly exaggerated, and that unjustified fears of genetic engineering have seriously impeded the development of valuable new drugs and therapies.

Yet while many Americans believe the risks and fears of genetic engineering have been exaggerated, they also express concern about them. Many survey respondents have agreed with statements such as "the potential danger from genetically altered cells and microbes is so great that strict regulations are necessary."

It appears that the public recognizes both the unreasonable fears associated with biotechnology as well as real risks. The former are seen as having delayed significant benefits from this technology. But the public still comes down on the side of strict regulation of the field, because it perceives potential dangers from the innovations.

While relatively few members of the general public can articulate any type of specific dangers about which they have heard or read, many believe that genetically engineered products are at least somewhat likely to represent a serious danger to humans or the environment. Such perceived dangers include:

the creation of antibiotic-resistant diseases
the production of birth defects in humans
the creation of herbicide-resistant weeds
the endangerment of the food supply
the environmental release of organisms that mutate into a
    deadly disease
the change of rainfall patterns
and an increase in the rate of plant or animal extinction

THINKING CREATIVELY

Being sympathetic to the real and imagined fears expressed in public opinion polls and having the talent to respond to them are not the only exercises of abstract thinking you can expect as a future biotechnologist. You will be called upon to visualize many things that, on the surface, laypeople might think to be products of unbridled free thought bordering on science fiction. In reality, they are the results of care and scientific expertise.

Some biotechnologists follow a step-by-step progression and think in an orderly fashion as they move to complete their research projects. Others work best when they experience flashes of insight. It is equally acceptable in this field to methodically heed all the conventional instructions when you work with your laboratory instruments as it is to "play around" with your instruments as you experimentally follow your educated instincts to achieve assigned goals.

ACCEPTING FAILURE

Regardless of your approach, you must be ready and willing to accept failure. It comes along very often. True, it is hard to take. The joys of success, however, equal or exceed the sorrows of falling short of your expectations. You will not advance in your career if the way you think and act is hindered by an apprehension of faltering. It is not wise to think nothing is happening just because nothing is happening immediately.

Sometimes, your work may seem to be dragging on a slow, day-to-day basis. Spark your excitement with the knowledge that you are heading in the right direction to create something that will be helpful to humanity.

You may be hearing about or actually confronting desperate individuals pleading for cures and treatments if you are specializing your efforts in disease research. Public pressure should not foster shortcuts, compromise, and haste in the research laboratory. Testing and retesting until the time is right for scientific acceptance should be part of the biotechnologist's creed.

The various aspects of temperament discussed in this chapter could be characterized as the little things that, when blended together, make a biotechnologist candidate more likely to move up the ladder in his or her chosen field. Paying attention to all these extras often may spell the difference between your having a bright future or none at all in the field of biotechnology.

CHAPTER 8

FINDING THE RIGHT JOB
IN BIOTECHNOLOGY

Do you believe that you want to spend your professional life in biotechnology? If so, this chapter will have special meaning for you.

Many tried and tested ways to secure employment are known to job seekers looking for work outside of biotechnology. Everyone who has experienced "the search" certainly appreciates the value of classified ads, phone calls, copy machines that are used for reproduction of work histories, postage stamps, Internet job searches, and, above all, a hearty supply of perseverance and hope. There is a better way to become a biotechnologist. Some of the following techniques are applicable only to this field, which, as you have seen, is a very unique one in many respects.

Recruiters are not necessarily the best resource for entry-level jobs. They are most useful when companies want to find experienced professionals who presently are doing their work at other companies.

Most firms have well-developed human resources departments. Unfortunately because numerous resumes are usually sitting in someone's in-box, there is not a simple way to get your resume and application noticed right away.

INITIATING A JOB SEARCH

Finding a Job by Networking

Perhaps the best way to make immediate contacts in the entry-level job marketplace is to network with individuals who are responsible for hiring at their companies. One way to find these key people is to go to the library and review scientific literature (books, magazines) for names, telephone numbers, and any other appropriate information about published authors in the industry. Another is to search relevant web sites on the Internet. Even though your contacts with these individuals will be seemingly cold calls on the telephone or by letters, you may find they will warm up to what you are attempting to do. After all, they were in the same position as you at one time, too. They are likely to give you a few names of who is doing what at their company.

Communicating with Contacts

Next, you should send a narrative cover letter to the contacts you have made. These notes should have pertinent elements. Mention what career directions you want to take, why you would be a plus in a biotechnology organization, and a little about where you want to go with your life in industry. The letter does not have to be long. Make it two or three paragraphs. Be sure it is well written.

There are many experts who recommend having a resume. An entry-level person should concentrate on its style, form, and how well it is written.

It is easy to spot a professionally written resume created in a resume shop. It is better for you to develop a resume yourself. Focus upon your goals rather than what you have done in the past. Make sure that all the information you include is relevant. Leave out information about hobbies and extracurricular activities, such as voluntary church work. Companies are interested in seeing information about your potential commercial value to them. They will appreciate information about your education, special skills, and any research experience you have gained.

There is nothing wrong about preparing your resume on a computer and changing certain aspects of the text several times to fit the operational requirements of different companies. You may, for instance, have an interest in being involved in large-scale mammalian cell culture and working for a production house that manufactures pharmaceuticals. On the other hand, you may consider it rewarding to sell the instrumentation that does this process. Your overall job statement should be very specific.

Make follow-up telephone calls to these people as your next step. You will find that 60 to 70 percent of them will make themselves available to you after they receive your letter.

One good way to give yourself credibility when you are at entry level without any professional experience is to use the credentials of your professors. Most of the time, these university faculty members are networking along industry lines anyway. Some companies ask professors to report to them the names of top students who are getting diplomas from schools of higher learning.

Be realistic about the level of jobs you are qualified for initially. The kind of letter that states, "I want to be research director of your company," is the kind of letter that will be disregarded by employers. You must show in your letter an aggressive interest and enthusiasm about what the company does. Indicate that you are ready to come in on the ground-floor level as a technician.

You do not want your letter to look like one that is being sent off to many different companies. Hiring officials can quickly spot a letter that appears to have been mass produced by a resume service. That is why it is very important that you bring up specific things about yourself and the company in which you are interested.

SUCCEEDING IN AN INTERVIEW

Phone Interviews

Some biotechnology companies do their initial interviewing over the telephone. Therefore, develop your telephone skills. This includes predetermining the time when someone is going to call. Make certain you have notes that will help you with your role in the conversation. Ask intelligent questions since you do not have a great deal of experience about which to talk. Mention your career goals. Check company literature, the trade press, and the business press to find information about the company's products, its customers, its rank in the industry, and its current plans. Have all this "spontaneous" conversation pretty well rehearsed so it flows well on the telephone.

The company spokesperson to whom you will be talking first most likely will be a scientist who needs a technician and who thought your cover letter looked interesting. You would be surprised how many scientists feel uncomfortable in telephone interviews. So there is no reason why your conversation should not be two sided in terms of the questions being asked.

Send out as many letters as possible to a variety of companies. Recruiters say that it sometimes takes up to five interviews with various job candidates before one individual is tendered an invitation to join a staff. The process could take a long time.

In-Person Interviews

Scientists do have the authority to hire people. Sometimes job applicants will get a second telephone call from the company's human resources department. This person may be putting together the details for an in-person appearance at the home office. The trip is usually at the firm's expense.

The entry-level interview is typical of those in other industries. If you are a job candidate with a bachelor's degree and have no previous experience working in the biotechnology field, you can expect to spend some time at the human resources department filling out forms. You will get a complete orientation regarding the past, present, and future of your host company. You will tour the facilities and meet some of the people in the firm's groups.

Many companies in biotechnology have a laid-back, short-sleeved attitude. Quite a few of the employees you will see are casual in their appearance. Do not let that informality fool you, however. For instance, companies frown upon anyone who comes to a job interview ungroomed and in attire less than businesslike. Your clothing and hair are very important. These factors will be weighed along with your intellectual promise.

Above all, keep in mind that biotechnology firms are entrepreneurial enterprises. You will have to convince hiring officials that you are serious about your future and that of their company. The founders of these firms worked long hours. Do not be surprised if you are called upon to do the same.

It is crucial that you emphasize how you are going to benefit the company. Slant your goals to coincide with those of the firm and, even more specifically, with those of the person who is interviewing you.

Here is an overlooked technique you can use for your gain at the job interview. Listen for certain descriptive words that the interviewer uses when he or she talks about designated staff members or projects. For instance, an interviewer might constantly refer to members of the company research team as innovative or creative. Try to use these adjectives when you describe your past work. This is a subtle but effective way to build rapport.

Watch how you sit in your chair. Note the body language of the interviewer. If he or she is leaning forward at a point in the conversation, you do it, too. There is a strong psychological plus on the subconscious level that comes into play here. You are making the person across the desk aware that, in a sense, you are like him or her. However, do not get so occupied with picking up on the interviewer's mannerisms that you lose track of what is being said to you.

The following are other things to do during a job interview that all contribute to enhancing your image and your chances of being added to the company's roster:

- Smile when it is natural to do so.
- Be courteous to everyone with whom you come into contact at the company.
- Try to maintain eye contact with your interviewer.
- Do not sit perfectly still. It is acceptable to be somewhat animated, when appropriate, with your head, eyes, and hands.
- Always tell the truth.

As an entry-level job candidate, you should control the conversation about 40 percent of the time. It makes you look good when you show enough interest in your future employer to ask questions about his or her company's history and its future potential. These queries should be planned and reviewed in advance. Many hiring officials decide upon the worth of job applicants by the quality of the questions they ask.

Once you have completed your job interview, you will have to wait while company officials consider your chances for employment. You can anticipate a quick decision.

WORKING WITH RECRUITERS

It is common to change from one aspect of biotechnology into some other area of specialization. There is a great deal of horizontal movement in the areas of operations, manufacturing, quality control, and regulatory affairs. People move back and forth between all of these disciplines.

When a person already is in the biotechnology business and is planning a career move within the industry, recruiters can be most helpful. There is a variety of different "head hunters" out there. They fill job assignments that companies give them. This accounts for 80 percent of their activities.

If you bring yourself, for example, to the attention of a recruiter who is impressed with you, he or she will go to bat for you, making contacts on your behalf with the objective of making a placement.

A good recruiter screens his or her clients. The thing that is important to a recruiter is the client's seriousness in making a move. The recruiter will want to establish why an individual wants to leave one job for another.

Recruiters are not running employment agencies. They do not charge people fees for doing things for them. Companies pay that expense, because they want to learn what personnel prospects are out there.

If someone wants to make a move within the biotechnology industry without the aid of a recruiter, there is always the danger of jeopardizing confidentiality somewhere down the road. While that person is busy introducing himself or herself, word gets around. There is a chance that his or her present employer will learn of the job search. Recruiters, on the other hand, will call as many companies as it takes without releasing an individual's name.

The best way to contact a recruiter is to look in trade magazines, industry listings, and material put out by trade associations. You can scan membership lists of these organizations (if available) and, without difficulty, pick out which ones are recruiters. Associates at your present job might know some names of recruiters, too.

The big corporate names in the industry will have well-developed human resources departments. They might even go on campus to look for employees.

Everyone has opinions regarding whether it is better to work for a small company or a large one. Your personality type will determine what is right for you. If you enjoy being surrounded by the trappings of a large company that offers outstanding benefits, that is good. Conversely, you might like to "wear all types of hats" and be able to experience rapid career growth. You will be able to achieve this in all probability at a small company.

A nice thing about biotechnology is that you can choose your own career options. It is truly a ground floor opportunity today, and, the way it looks, things will get even better.

BIOTECHNOLOGY TIME LINE

The Biotechnology Industry Organization (BIO) has compiled a time line of developments in biotechnology. The following is a condensed version of that list.

1750 B.C.
- The Sumerians brew beer.

500 B.C.
- The Chinese use moldy soybean curds as an antibiotic to treat boils.

A.D. 100
- Powdered chrysanthemum is used in China as an insecticide.

1590
- The microscope is invented by Janssen.

1663
- Cells are first described by Hooke.

1675
- Leeuwenhoek discovers bacteria.

1797

- Jenner inoculates a child with a viral vaccine to protect him from smallpox.

1830

- Proteins are discovered.

1833

- The first enzymes are isolated.

1855

- The *Escherichia coli (E. coli)* bacterium is discovered. It later becomes a major research, development, and production tool for biotechnology.

1863

- Mendel, in his study of peas, discovers that traits are transmitted from parents to progeny by discrete, independent units, later called genes. His observations laid the groundwork for the field of genetics.

1869

- Miescher discovers DNA in the sperm of trout.

1877

- A technique for staining and identifying bacteria is developed by Koch.

1878

- The first centrifuge is developed by Laval.

1879
- Fleming discovers chromatin, the rodlike structures inside the cell nucleus that later came to be called chromosomes.
- In Michigan, Darwin devotee William James Beal makes the first clinically controlled crosses of corn in search of colossal yields.

1900
- Drosophila (fruit flies) are used in early studies of genes.

1902
- The term "immunology" first appears.

1906
- The term "genetics" is introduced.

1911
- The first cancer-causing virus is discovered by Rous.

1914
- Bacteria are used to treat sewage for the first time in Manchester, England.

1915
- Phages, or bacterial viruses, are discovered.

1919
- The word "biotechnology" is first used by a Hungarian agricultural engineer.

1920
- The human growth hormone is discovered by Evans and Long.

1928
- Fleming discovers penicillin, the first antibiotic.

1938
- The term "molecular biology" is coined.

1940
- American Oswald Avery demonstrates that DNA is the "transforming factor" and is the material of genes.

1941
- The term "genetic engineering" is first used by Danish microbiologist A. Jost in a lecture on sexual reproduction in yeast at the Technical Institute in Lwow, Poland.

1942
- The electron microscope is used to identify and characterize a bacteriophage—a virus that infects bacteria.

1944
- Waksman isolates streptomycin, an effective antibiotic for TB.

1946
- Discovery is made that genetic material from different viruses can be combined to form a new type of virus, an example of genetic recombination.

1947

- McClintock discovers transposable elements, or "jumping genes," in corn.

1949

- Pauling shows that sickle cell anemia is a "molecular disease" resulting from a mutation in the protein molecule hemoglobin.

1950

- Artificial insemination of livestock using frozen semen (a longtime dream many of farmers) is successfully accomplished.

1953

- Nature publishes James Watson's and Francis Crick's manuscript describing the double helical structure of DNA, which marks the beginning of the modern era of genetics.

1954

- Cell-culturing techniques are developed.

1955

- An enzyme involved in the synthesis of a nucleic acid is isolated for the first time.

1956

- The fermentation process is perfected in Japan. Kornberg discovers the enzyme DNA polymerase I, leading to an understanding of how DNA is replicated.

1958

- Sickle cell anemia is shown to occur due to a change of a single amino acid.

1959

- Systemic fungicides are developed. The steps in protein biosynthesis are delineated.

Also in the 1950s:
- Discovery of interferons is made.
- First synthetic antibiotic is produced.

1960

- Exploiting base pairing, hybrid DNA-RNA molecules are created.
- Messenger RNA is discovered.

1964

- The International Rice Research Institute in the Philippines starts the Green Revolution with new strains of rice that double the yield of previous strains if given sufficient fertilizer.

1965

- Harris and Watkins successfully fuse mouse and human cells.

1966

- The genetic code is cracked, demonstrating that a sequence of three nucleotide bases (a condon) determines each of twenty amino acids.

1967

- The first automatic protein sequencer is perfected.

1969

- An enzyme is synthesized *in vitro* for the first time.

1970

- Specific restriction nucleases are identified, opening the way for gene cloning.
- First complete synthesis of a gene occurs.

1971

- Discovery is made of restriction enzymes that cut and splice genetic material.

1972

- The DNA composition of humans is discovered to be 99 percent similar to that of chimpanzees and gorillas.
- Initial work with embryo transfer occurs.

1973

- Stanley Cohen and Herbert Boyer perfect genetic engineering techniques to cut and paste DNA (using restriction enzymes and ligases) and reproduce the new DNA in bacteria.

1974

- The National Institutes of Health forms a Recombinant DNA Advisory Committee to oversee recombinant genetic research.

1975

- Asilomar Conference (moratorium on genetic engineering research) is held.
- The first monoclonal antibodies are produced.

1976

- The tools of recombinant DNA are first applied to a human inherited disorder.
- Molecular hybridization is used for the prenatal diagnosis of alpha thalassemia.
- Yeast genes are expressed in *E. coli* bacteria.
- DNA sequencing is discovered; first working synthetic gene.

1977

- First expression of human gene in bacteria occurs.
- Methods for reading DNA sequence using electrophoresis are discovered.

1978

- High-level structure of virus is first identified.
- Recombinant human insulin is first produced.
- North Carolina scientists show it is possible to introduce specific mutations at specific sites in a DNA molecule.

1979

- Human growth hormone is first synthesized.

1980

- The U.S. Supreme Court, in the landmark case Diamond *v.* Chakrabarty, approves the principle of patenting

genetically engineered life-forms, which allows the Exxon Oil Company to patent an oil-eating microorganism.
- The U.S. patent for gene cloning is awarded to Cohen and Boyer.
- The first gene-synthesizing machines are developed.
- Researchers successfully introduce a human gene—one that codes for the protein interferon—into a bacterium.

1981
- Scientists at Ohio University produce the first transgenic animals by transferring genes from other animals into mice.
- Chinese scientist becomes the first to clone a fish—a golden carp.

1982
- Applied Biosystems, Inc., introduces the first commercial gas phase protein sequencer, dramatically reducing the amount of protein sample needed for sequencing.

1983
- The Polymerase Chain Reaction (PCR) technique is conceived. PCR, which uses heat and enzymes to make unlimited copies of genes and gene fragments, later becomes a major tool in biotech research and product development worldwide.
- The first genetic transformation of plant cells by TI plasmids is performed.
- The first artificial chromosome is synthesized.

- The first genetic markers for specific inherited diseases are found.

1984

- The DNA fingerprinting technique is developed.
- The first genetically engineered vaccine is developed.
- The entire genome of HIV is cloned and sequenced.

1985

- Genetic marking is found for kidney disease and cystic fibrosis.
- Genetic fingerprinting enters the courtroom.
- Genetically engineered plants resistant to insects, viruses, and bacteria are field tested for the first time.
- The NIH approves guidelines for performing experiments in gene therapy on humans.

1986

- University of California, Berkeley, chemist describes how to combine antibodies and enzymes (abzymes) to create pharmaceuticals.
- The first field tests of genetically engineered plants (tobacco) are conducted.
- The Environmental Protection Agency approves the release of the first genetically engineered crop—gene-altered tobacco plants.

1987

- First field trials of a genetically altered bacterium occur.

- Frostban, a genetically altered bacterium that inhibits frost formation on crop plants, is field tested on strawberry and potato plants in California, the first authorized outdoor tests of an engineered bacterium.
- Treatments are approved for heart attacks and hepatitis C.

1988

- Harvard molecular geneticists are awarded the first U.S. patent for a genetically altered animal—a transgenic mouse.
- A patent for a process to make bleach-resistant protease enzymes to use in detergents is awarded.
- Congress funds the Human Genome Project, a massive effort to map and sequence the human genetic code as well as the genomes of other species.

1989

- First field trial of a recombinant viral crop protectant occurs.
- The gene responsible for cystic fibrosis is discovered.

1990

- An artificially produced form of chymosin, an enzyme for cheese-making, is introduced. It is the first product of recombinant DNA technology in the U.S. food supply.
- Human Genome Project—an international effort to map all of the genes in the human body—is launched.
- The first federally approved gene therapy treatment is performed successfully on a four-year-old girl suffering from an immune disorder.

- The first successful field trial of genetically engineered cotton plants is conducted. The plants had been engineered to withstand use of the herbicide Bromoxynil.
- The first transgenic dairy cow—used to produce human milk proteins for infant formula—is created.

1991

- Neupogen® is approved for the treatment of low white blood cells in chemotherapy patients.
- Leukine®, used to replenish white blood cell counts after bone marrow transplants, is approved.

1992

- Proleukin® is approved for the treatment of renal cell cancer.
- American and British scientists unveil a technique for testing embryos *in vitro* for genetic abnormalities such as cystic fibrosis and hemophilia.

1993

- The FDA declares that genetically engineered foods are "not inherently dangerous" and do not require special regulation.
- The Biotechnology Industry Organization (BIO) is created by merging two smaller trade associations.

1994

- The FLAVRSAVR™ tomato—the first genetically engineered whole food approved by the FDA—is on the market.
- The first breast cancer gene is discovered.

1995

- The first baboon-to-human bone marrow transplant is performed on an AIDS patient.
- The first full gene sequence of a living organism other than a virus is completed for the bacterium *Hemophilus influenzae*.
- Gene therapy, immune system modulation, and genetically engineered antibodies enter the clinics in the war against cancer.

1996

- The discovery of a gene associated with Parkinson's disease provides an important new avenue of research into the cause and potential treatment of the debilitating neurological ailment.
- AlphaNine® SD is approved to prevent and control bleeding in patients with Factor IX deficiency due to *hemophilia B*.
- DaunoXome® is approved as a first-line treatment for HIV-related Kaposi's sarcoma.
- Fertinex™ is approved for treatment of female infertility to stimulate ovulation disorders and in women undergoing assisted reproductive technologies treatment.

1997

- Scottish scientists report cloning a sheep, named Dolly, using DNA from adult sheep cells.
- A group of Oregon researchers claims to have cloned two rhesus monkeys.

- A new DNA technique combines PCR, DNA chips, and a computer program, providing a new tool in the search for disease-causing genes.
- Carticel™ is approved for treatment of knee cartilage damage.
- Prandin is approved as an antidiabetic agent for treatment of type 2 diabetes.

1998
- University of Hawaii scientists clone three generations of mice from the nuclei of adult ovarian cumulus cells.
- Embryonic stem cells can be used to regenerate tissue and create disorders mimicking diseases.
- Scientists at Japan's Kinki University clone eight identical calves using cells taken from a single adult cow.
- The first complete animal genome for the elegans worm is sequenced.
- A rough draft of the human genome map is produced, showing the locations of more than thirty thousand genes.
- PROVIGIL® is approved to improve wakefulness in patients with excessive daytime sleepiness (EDS) associated with narcolepsy.
- IntegrilinÖ is approved for treatment of patients with acute coronary syndrome and angioplasty.

Also in the 1990s:
- First conviction is made using genetic fingerprinting in the United Kingdom.

- The gene that clearly participates in the normal process of regulating weight is isolated.
- Discovery that hereditary colon cancer is caused by defective DNA repair gene is made.
- Genetically engineered rabies vaccine is tested in raccoons.
- Genetically engineered biopesticide is approved for sale in the United States.
- Patents are issued for mice with specific transplanted genes.
- First European patent is issued for a genetically engineered mouse that is sensitive to carcinogens.
- Breast cancer susceptibility genes are cloned.

SELECTED SCHOOLS OFFERING BIOTECHNOLOGY PROGRAMS

University of British Columbia
2329 West Mall
Vancouver, BC
Canada V6T 1Z4

University of Calgary
2500 University Drive NW
Calgary, AB
Canada T2N 1N4

Colorado Institute of Research in Biotechnology
University of Colorado
Department of Chemical Engineering
Boulder, CO 80309

Dalhousie University
Halifax, Nova Scotia
Canada B3H 3J5

Foothill College
12345 El Monte Road
Los Altos, CA 94022-4599

Georgia Institute of Technology
Atlanta, GA 30332-0230

University of Illinois Biotechnology Center
901 South Mathews Avenue
Urbana, IL 61801

Madison Area Technical College
  Biotechnology Program
  3550 Anderson Street
  Madison, WI 53704-2599

University of Maryland
  College of Life Sciences
  1109 Microbiology Building
  College Park, MD 20742

McGill University
  Lakeshore Road
  Ste. Anne de Bellevue,
  Montreal, Quebec
  Canada H9X 3V9

University of Missouri-St. Louis
  R223 Research Building
  8001 Natural Bridge Road
  St. Louis, MO 63121

Montgomery College
  51 Mannakee Street
  Rockville, MD 20850

University of Montreal
  Montreal, Quebec
  Canada H3T 1P1

Northwestern University Center for Biotechnology
  BIRL
  1801 Maple Avenue
  Evanston, IL 60201

University of Pennsylvania
  Towne Building, Room 111
  University of Pennsylvania
  Philadelphia, PA 19104

University of Texas-Stephen F. Austin University
  The University of Texas Health Center
  11937 U.S. Highway 271
  Tyler, TX 75708

Virginia Tech
  Fralin Biotechnology Center
  Blacksburg, VA 24061

University of Toronto
  Toronto, Ontario
  Canada M5S 1A1

University of Wisconsin-River Falls
  410 South Third Street
  River Falls, WI 54022

BIOTECHNOLOGY ASSOCIATIONS

Following are addresses of a number of biotechnology associations.

Canada

Industrial Biotechnology Association of Canada
130 Albert Street, Suite 420
Ottawa, ON
Canada, K1P 5G4

United States

Biotechnology Industry Organization (BIO)
1625 K Street NW, Suite 1100
Washington, DC 20006

BIO STATE AFFILIATES

Arkansas

Arkansas Biotechnology Association
C/O 4301 West Markem
Little Rock, AR 72205

California

Bay Area Bioscience Center
311 California Street, Suite 610
San Francisco, CA 94104

BIOCOM/San Diego
4510 Executive Drive
San Diego, CA 92121

California Health Care Institute
1020 Prospect Street, Suite 310
La Jolla, CA 92037

Colorado

Colorado Biotechnology Association
6755 South Ivy Way
Englewood, CO 80112

Connecticut

Connecticut United for Research Excellence
175 Capital Boulevard
Rocky Hill, CT 06067

Florida

BioFlorida
15205 SW Seventy-Eighth Court
Miami, FL 33157

Georgia

Georgia Biomedical Partnership
285 Peachtree Center Avenue NE
Marquis Two Tower, Suite 1100
Atlanta, GA 30303

Iowa

Iowa Biotechnology Association
1200 Valley West Drive
West Des Moines, IA 50266

Maine

Biotechnology Association of Maine
   P. O. Box 646
   168 Capitol Street
   Augusta, ME 04333

Maryland

Maryland Bioscience Alliance
   9700 Great Seneca Highway
   Rockville, MD 20850

Massachusetts

Massachusetts Biotechnology Council
   One Cambridge Center, 4th Floor
   Cambridge, MA 02142

Michigan

Michigan Biotechnology Association
   1400 Abbott Road, Suite 310
   East Lansing, MI 48823

Minnesota

Minnesota Biotechnology Association
   26 East Exchange Street, Suite 500
   St. Paul, MN 55101

New Jersey

Biotechnology Council of New Jersey
   160 West State Street
   Trenton, NJ 08608

New York

New York Biotechnology Association
   25 East Loop Road, Suite 203
   Stony Brook, NY 11790

North Carolina

North Carolina Bioscience Organization
2100 First Union Capitol Center
150 Fayettville Street Mall
Raleigh, NC 27601

Ohio

Edison Biotechnology Center
3845 Hillbrook Road
University Heights, OH 44118

Oregon

Oregon Biosciences Association
2611 SW Third Street, Suite 200
Portland, OR 97201

Pennsylvania

Pennsylvania Biotechnology Association
20 Valley Stream Parkway
Malvern, PA 19355

South Carolina

South Carolina Biotechnology Association
3406 Richland Avenue West
Aiken, SC 29801

Tennessee

Tennessee Biotechnology Association
501 Fifth Street
Bristol, TN 37620

Texas

Texas Healthcare & Bioscience Institute
815 Brazos, Suite 310
Austin, TX 78701

Utah

Utah Life Science Industries Association
  P. O. Box 58073
  Salt Lake City, UT 84158

Virginia

Virginia Biotechnology Association
  P. O. Box 2020
  Louisa, VA 23093

Washington

Washington Biotechnology & Biomedical Association
  1100 Olive Way, Suite 300
  Seattle, WA 98101

Wisconsin

Wisconsin Biotechnology Association
  505 South Rosa Road
  Madison, WI 53717

GLOSSARY

The following is a condensed version of a glossary provided courtesy of the Biotechnology Industry Organization.

Acclimatization.   Adaptation of an organism to a new environment.

Active immunity.   A type of acquired immunity whereby resistance to a disease is built up by either having the disease or receiving a vaccine to it.

Adjuvant.   Insoluble material that increases the formation and persistence of antibodies when injected with an antigen.

Aerobic.   Needing oxygen for growth.

Alielle.   Any of several alternative forms of a gene.

Allogenic.   Of the same species, but with a different genotype.

Amino acids.   Building blocks of proteins. There are twenty common amino acids: alanine, arginine, aspargine, aspartic acid, cysteine, glutamic acid, glutamine, glycine, histidine, isoleucine, leucine, lysine, methionine, phenylalanine, proline, serine, threonine, tryptophan, tyrosine, and valine.

Amplification.   The process of increasing the number of copies of a particular gene or chromosomal sequence.

Anaerobic.   Growing in the absence of oxygen.

Antibody.   Protein produced by humans and higher animals in response to the presence of a specific antigen.

Antigen.   A substance that, when introduced into the body, induces an immune response by a specific antibody.

Autoimmune disease.   A disease in which the body produces antibodies against its own tissues.

Bioassay.   Determination of the effectiveness of a compound by measuring its effect on animals, tissues, or organisms in comparison with a standard preparation.

Biocatalyst.   In bioprocessing, an enzyme that activates or speeds up a biochemical reaction.

Biochemical.   The product of a chemical reaction in a living organism.

Biochip.   An electronic device that uses organic molecules to form a semiconductor.

Biodegradable.   Capable of being reduced to water and carbon dioxide by the action of microorganisms.

Biomaterials.   Biological molecules, such as proteins and complex sugars, used to make medical devices, including structural elements used in reconstructive surgery.

Bioprocess.   A process in which living cells, or components thereof, are used to produce a desired product.

Biosynthesis.   Production of a chemical by a living organism.

Biotechnology.   Development of products by a biological process. Production may be carried out by using intact organisms, such as yeasts and bacteria, or by using natural substances (e.g., enzymes) from organisms.

Callus. A cluster of undifferentiated plant cells that can, in some species, be induced to form the whole plant.

Carcinogen. Cancer-causing agent.

Catalyst. An agent (such as an enzyme or a metallic complex) that facilitates a reaction but is not itself changed during the reaction.

Cell culture. Growth of cells under laboratory conditions.

Chromosomes. Threadlike components in the cell that contain DNA and proteins. Genes are carried on the chromosomes.

Co-metabolism. A microbe oxidizing not only its main energy source but also another organic compound.

Crossing over. Exchange of genes between two paired chromosomes.

Cyto-. Referring to cell or cell plasm.

Cytogenetics. Study of the cell and its heredity-related components, especially chromosomes.

Cytoplasm. Cellular material that is within the cell membrane and surrounds the nucleus.

Deoxyribonucleic acid (DNA). The molecule that carries the genetic acid information for most living systems.

DNA sequence. The order of nucleotide bases in the DNA molecule.

Enzyme. A protein catalyst that facilitates specific chemical or metabolic reactions necessary for cell growth and reproduction.

Eukaryote. A cell or organism containing a true nucleus, with a well-defined membrane surrounding the nucleus. All organisms except bacteria, viruses, and blue-green algae are eukaryotic.

Feedstock. The raw material used for chemical or biological processes.

Fusion. Joining of the membrane of two cells, thus creating a daughter cell that contains some of the same properties from each parent cells.

Gene. A segment of chromosome. Some genes direct the syntheses of proteins, while other have regulatory functions.

Gene mapping. Determination of the relative locations of genes on a chromosome.

Genetic engineering. A technology used to alter the genetic material of living cells in order to make them capable of producing new substances or performing new functions.

Genome. The total hereditary material of a cell, comprising the entire chromosomal set found in each nucleus of a given species.

Germplasm. The total genetic variability, represented by germ cells or seeds, available to a particular population of organisms.

Haploid. A cell with half the usual number of chromosomes, or only one chromosome set.

Heredity. Transfer of genetic information from parent cells to progeny.

Host. A cell or organism used for growth of a virus, plasmid, or other form of foreign DNA, or for the production of clones substances.

Immune response. The response of the immune system to challenge by a foreign antigen.

Immune serum. Blood serum containing antibodies.

Immunoassay. Technique for identifying substances based on the use of antibodies.

Immunogen. Any substance that can elicit an immune response.

Immunology. Study of all phenomena related to the body's response to antigenic challenge.

In situ. Treatment of a hazardous waste site entailing no excavation or removal of soil or water.

In vitro. Literally, "in glass." Performed in a test tube or other laboratory apparatus.

In vivo. In the living organism.

Library. A set of cloned DNA fragments.

Linker. A fragment of DNA with a restriction site that can be used to join DNA strands.

Medium. A substance containing nutrients needed for cell growth.

Metabolism. All biochemical activities carried out by an organism to maintain life.

Microbiology. Study of living organisms that can be seen only under a microscope.

Molecular genetics. Study of how genes function to control cellular activities.

Mutation. A change in the genetic material of a cell.

Nucleus. The structure within eukaryotic cells that contains chromosomal DNA.

Organic compound. A compound containing carbon.

Pathogen. Disease-causing organism.

Peptide. Two or more amino acids joined by a linkage called a peptide bond.

Polymer. A long molecule of repeated subunits.

Prokaryote. An organism (e.g., bacterium, virus, blue-green algae) whose DNA is not enclosed within a nuclear membrane.

Protein. A molecule composed of amino acids.

Reagent. Substance used in a chemical reaction.

Replication.   Reproduction or duplication, as of an exact copy of a strand of DNA.

Repressor.   A protein that binds to an operator adjacent to a structural gene, inhibiting transcription of that gene.

Ribosome.   A cellular component, containing protein and RNA, that is involved in protein synthesis.

Scale-up.   Transition from small-scale production to production of large industrial quantities.

Selective medium.   Nutrient material constituted such that it will support the growth of specific organisms while inhibiting the growth of others.

Structural gene.   A gene that codes for a protein, such as an enzyme.

Suppressor gene.   A gene that can reverse the effect of a mutation in other genes.

Technology transfer.   The process of transferring discoveries made by basic research institutions, such as universities and government laboratories, to the commercial sector for development into useful products and services.

Tissue culture.   *In vitro* growth in nutrient medium of cells isolated from tissue.

Toxin.   A poisonous substance produced by certain microorganisms or plants.

Virology.   Study of viruses.

Virus.   A submicroscopic organism that contains genetic information but cannot reproduce itself. To replicate, it must invade another cell and use parts of that cell's reproductive machinery.